Island of the Lost

ISLAND

BY THE SAME AUTHOR: *Tal*

Paul Fenimore Cooper

OF THE LOST

FOUNDED 1838

GPPS

G. P. PUTNAM'S SONS   NEW YORK

To Babbie and Niki
*who three times flew with
me to King William Island*

Author's Note

This is the story of a far-off arctic island—King William Island —and of what has happened there since the time of the island's rise from the sea just after the last Ice Age down to the present. It tells of the giants who first lived on the island, of the Eskimos who drove them off, and of the explorers who went to the island in the nineteenth and twentieth centuries. Always in the background is the island itself, really the heroine of the book. Around her I have tried to weave the fascination and the wonder and the strangeness that the North has always held for me, even as a child.

In gratitude to those who helped with the book—in leading me to source material, in the field, and in the writing itself—I wish to thank Richard J. Cyriax, Margaret Follett, Wilson Follett, Father Pierre Henry, Vilhjalmur Stefansson and Charles A. Weber. Also, I wish to acknowledge the kindness of the Smithsonian Institution in making available the Hall journals and notebooks, details from which have added much to Chapters 2, 4, and 7 of Part III.

PAUL FENIMORE COOPER

Cooperstown, N. Y.

Contents

PART I
The Island Is Born

1.

To the Eskimos it was always Kikerktak—the island. Later white men called it King William Land, then King William Island. Its story, like a fairy tale, begins in a far-off time, when the last Ice Age was drawing to a close. The vast northlands of America lay bare and flat and lifeless, scraped clean by the once advancing ice. Now this ice had receded, leaving behind it thousands of sparkling lakes. A huge new bay marked the spot where the ocean had leaked in to fill a broad depression in the land. Great new rivers wound their ways across the Barren Lands to the Polar Sea, which then extended much farther south than today and washed over pressed-down lands that would later rise to dryness again.

With the weight of the ice gone, the earth's crust began to move upwards. It was a slow rising, no more than six feet in a hundred years; but it was steady and persistent. In time it added thousands of square miles of new land to the continent; and it created hundreds of islands in the waters to the north—today's great Arctic Archipelago.

Among these islands was Kikerktak. It rose fresh and untouched from the sea; not all at once as the goddess of beauty did, but through thousands of years. It still bears the marks of its origin. Even now, everywhere on Kikerktak, there are sea shells; the bleached bones of whales lie on ridges two hundred feet above the sea and half a mile inland; and telltale strand lines show where the coast once was and mark its unhalting rise from the deep.

For a long time Kikerktak lay undiscovered. Grasses and flowers spread over the island. Salmon ran up rivers and streams; seal played in the waters of the surrounding sea; and thousands of birds came to the island to make their homes. Animals came, too—the caribou, the bear, the fox, and the lemming. The life that had been driven away by the Ice Age came back; only the arrival of man was awaited.

A thousand years or so ago—according to legend—a race of giants, the Tunrit, came to the island. Along its southern shore, close to the water's edge, they built stone houses with sod roofs held up by whalebones, and there they settled down to live. They were not long in finding out the migration paths of the caribou; and along the paths, at certain points, they built on the ridge tops stone pillars that the caribou apparently mistook for hunters and in trying to avoid them fell into ambushes and were killed. The Tunrit found where the caribou swam across the lakes and rivers, and in those places they pursued them and killed them with lances. They found the best streams for fishing and built stone dams and weirs to make the catching easier. Before long they had taken the whole island over and turned it into a home for themselves.

Their life was a good one. The land gave them the caribou, the streams the fish, and the sea the mammals of the deep, for then the waters around the island were less shallow and more open than today, and great monsters—whales and white whales and narwhals—traveled, in summer, along the coast.

These the Tunrit, in their kayaks, hunted to their hearts' content. Night never came to interrupt the chase. Only exhaustion or a mishap of some kind could bring the hunting to an end. When it was successful, the reward was great—oil in plenty, blubber in plenty, and bone for tools and weapons and utensils of every kind.

These Tunrit were a strange people, big and sturdy, yet stupid and easygoing. They did not know how to dress skins or make waterproof boots; and in many ways they were slovenly and filthy. They slept on sealskins with the blubber still attached; and under their jackets, next to their bodies, they kept meat until it was strong and rancid; then they ate it with appetite. They dressed in bearskin jackets and trousers that made them look woolly and even bigger than they were. They had a certain skill in the treatment of the sick; when one of them had a bad headache, a hole was drilled in his head, and relief gained by letting blood and matter ooze out.

Their strength was great. One of them could single-handedly pick up a bear and throw it over his shoulder or pull a walrus from the sea. They were long-legged and equal in fleetness to the caribou they ran down and killed with the lance. Often when in a rage, they struck their harpoons so forcibly against the rocks as to make a shower of stone splinters. They were skillful with the spear and had a way of kicking it from the top of the foot with such accurate aim as never to miss its mark. Even today a story is told of how one of the Tunrit in this fashion killed an Eskimo's dog as it ran along the shore of a lake.

How long these Tunrit stayed on Kikerktak, no one knows. All that is known is that they made the place suitable for living and that later Eskimos came and took the island away from them. It was the Tunrit's amiability and stupidity that proved their downfall. At first they let the Eskimos live on the island side by side with them, in peace. But quarrels soon arose, and before long the newcomers took to hunting the giants down like game. Now one, now two, they first separated from the others. These doomed ones were tracked until caught asleep; then the Eskimos quickly killed them by drilling holes in their foreheads. Still the Tunrit hung on, in the hope of coming to some agreement that would allow them to stay on Kikerktak. In the end the Eskimo abuse was too much; the Tunrit gave up and left the island for good. They fled to the north and to the east, swimming across wide stretches of water, laughing as they went; as often as not, when they reached the other side, they fell on the shore and died from exhaustion.

With the Tunrit out of the way, the Eskimos took over the island and have lived there ever since. They call themselves the Kikerktarmiut—the Island Dwellers; where they originally came from, they do not know. It is enough for them that their forefathers met the Tunrit and conquered them and drove them away. Why go back beyond such glorious deeds as those? Let us accept the Kikerktarmiut as they accept themselves, a race of giant killers from no one knows where, who took over an arctic island and made it their own.

Year after year the Kikerktarmiut, one of the Netsilingmiut group, followed a closely patterned life, doing each season exactly what their forefathers had done before them. In January, dressed in their new caribou clothing, they moved out onto the sea ice for months of hunting the seal at his breathing hole. Here, in their snow houses, they were truly the people of the North. But their life was far from ideal. It was all right when the sealing was good; then there was the fun of the hunt and the comfort of a full stomach and happiness all around. But even with the best of luck, the hunt did not always bring comfort and happiness. Often the hunting season was a time of disappointment and anxiety.

Many a time the sealing around Kikerktak failed; one year winter never came; the sea never froze over and it was impossible to hunt. That year people could get nothing to eat and were driven to the horrors of cannibalism. They covered the bodies of their dead with stones, as if hiding meat in a cache, and on this hidden store they lived. It was something to humble one's spirit; and those who were not reduced to it had the greatest pity and understanding for those who were. Ever after that winter those who had not been driven to cannibalism never offered the meat of bears or ravens to those unfortunate ones who had; it tasted too much like human flesh. It was the memory of such desperate times that haunted the hunter as he stood for long, cold hours by the breathing hole, waiting for the seal to come. He might wait a day or even two days, with no reward but failure. Food, however, had to be got; if one place did not provide it, another had to be tried. So the Kikerktarmiut were constantly on the move, giving up a poor hunting ground to look elsewhere for a better one.

This meant deserting their villages and taking all their possessions with them—their clothing, their sleeping skins and their domestic utensils. These were piled high on their sledges, and the strange procession moved off. Out in front were the men and the women and the dogs, all pulling together. Food was always so scarce that only a few dogs could be kept, just those needed for hunting, never enough also to do all the

pulling. Then came the loaded sledges; behind them the children who could walk, and last the old people in a straggle at
the rear. In this fashion, like the nomads they really were,
they wended their way across the frozen sea to a better hunting ground, where they built a new village of snow houses,
made new homes for themselves, and in a way began life all
over again.

For the Kikerktarmiut the winters were long and cold;
from January until May the temperature rarely rose above
zero. Most of the time, except in a mild year, the temperature
hovered between twenty and forty below, with occasional
brief drops to sixty below, or lower. Even when the days
were shortest, there were several hours of light bright enough
to see by. On January 17 the sun, after fifty-two days below
the horizon, came back to view. In the darkest of the winter
months the moon, around the time of full, was above the
horizon for four days and four nights at a stretch. No great
amount of snow fell, perhaps thirty inches in all; what did fall
stayed on the ground from one end of the season to the other.
It was not fluffy and soft as the snow farther south is but
fine and granular like sand and so hard packed by the winds
that it could be easily walked on. By the first of April the
nights were light; by the middle of May the cold was showing signs of moderating. In June the Kikerktarmiut abandoned
their snow houses on the ice and took up life on the land
again.

On Kikerktak June was the most wonderful month of all.
Already the midnight sun was high; there was warmth at
noon. With the beginning of the thaw winter visibly disappeared. The spots of bare ground grew bigger; the lakes melted
around the edges; where the streams flowed into the lakes

there were muddy splotches on the ice. Up and down the coast stretches of putty-colored limestone beach began to show, still ridged in many places with snow. Flocks of ducks and geese came back, followed later by swans; in the warmth of the sunlight was the promise of what lay ahead. Then, almost overnight, Kikerktak was transformed. The snow vanished, disclosing a flat land covered with a thousand lakes still frozen over. On the deeper lakes the ice often stayed until July. Between the lakes stretched the water-soaked tundra, its brown, clay soil thick and sticky. There was a golden tint to the grasses and the moss; in the swamps the wading birds were busy building their nests and laying their eggs. The snowy owl, perched on his great rock, waited for the unsuspecting lemming. There was water everywhere: it covered the ice on the lakes; it swelled in the rivulets and marshes; and it gurgled and splashed over the ridges down to the sea.

Tiny flowers began to bloom—red and yellow and white and blue. They were the descendants of plants that had survived the Ice Age and had spread again over the North. They were little flowers, like Alpines, but they bloomed in drifts, splashing their color across the land and adding their delicate beauty to it. Bees hummed over them and bright-colored butterflies floated by. It was a quick, sudden coming to full life; there was not much time to waste.

It was a wonder the fragile plants could survive at all; the air, even with spring coming, still had a wintry chill, and only a few inches below the surface the ground stayed frozen the year around. It was this that made vegetation possible. In frost-free ground the water would have sunk in and drained away and not have been held to form a reservoir from which the plants might drink. The one thing that seemed most against their survival had been turned to their advantage. Nature had made provision against the frosty air, too. The dark-colored surface soil and moss absorbed the sun's heat and held it, so that close to the earth the air was much warmer than higher up. Thus the plants had a covering of warm air; each was in a tiny hothouse of its own.

With summer at hand the Kikerktarmiut came in from the sea. The caribou were returning north, great herds of them, the cows with their newborn calves; soon the island hunting would begin. The snow house and the frozen sea were abandoned, and life was taken up in skin tents along the shores of the inland lakes. The Kikerktarmiut knew just where the caribou crossings were and just when the herds would pass by. Season after season the island dwellers re-enacted the drama their forefathers had acted before them. The kayak men waited for the beaters to drive the animals into the water, where they were easily overtaken and killed with lances. When the caribou came north at the beginning of summer they were lean; great numbers had to be slain for sufficient food, and their skins were useless for clothing. So the hunting went on, the weather grew even warmer, and to the natives Kikerktak became an earthly paradise.

By August the great fishing days had arrived, and everyone went to Lake Amitsoq in the center of the island. It was a long, narrow lake joined by a small stream to another lake. The trout, on their way from the upper lake to the lower one, could be trapped and killed in the stream with spears. Always there were plenty of them; a never-ending supply, it would seem. Because the place never failed to give food, it was regarded as holy—a spot where the spirits that ruled the world had chosen to show kindness toward man. The Eskimos came to it with joy and wonder in their hearts; to be at Amitsoq for the fishing was something not to be missed. Friends from afar met there year after year, and the days were happy from beginning to end. The catch was taken in the morning and again in the evening, leaving plenty of time between to play games and talk and visit. The children swam in the lake, and everywhere there was gaiety and fun.

Already, in August, the feel of winter was in the air, but it was not yet too late for warm, sunny days. On these the Eskimo basked and dreamed and let his life of endless toil slip out of mind. Then he allowed his fancy to play—and what a strange fancy it was! Driftwood came from the forests that grew at the bottom of the sea; storms broke off the branches and they floated to the surface. Down there, too, lived the Spirit of the Sea, the most powerful ruler in the world. Her name was Nuliajuk, and she had begun life as an orphan child in a village near an inlet on the west coast of Adelaide Peninsula—a part of the mainland opposite Kikerktak. One time, on rafts tied together, the people of this village were hurrying to the other side of the inlet to better hunting grounds. As the rafts pulled from shore, some of the children, among them Nuliajuk, jumped aboard. The other children had families to look out for them, but poor Nuliajuk had none; she was just a nuisance and in the way. So the villagers threw her overboard to drown; and when she reached up to save herself by holding on to the edge of the raft, they cut her fingers off to make her let go. The fingers fell in the water and turned into seals, and Nuliajuk herself sank to the bottom and became the Spirit of the Sea. From that time on she ruled over the sea beasts and the land beasts as well, and every animal that was hunted fell under her control. Thus she gained great power over mankind and was able to wreak revenge for being so despised and so cruelly treated; in time she became the most feared and most dreaded spirit in the world.

Up in the sky, too, there were wonderful things to dream about. A red sunset meant that an old man or woman had died. And the sun and the moon were more than just the heavenly bodies of today. They had once been a boy and a girl, a brother and sister, the children of a cruel mother who wanted to kill her own son. When she tried, she failed; instead the sister helped the brother, and together they killed their own mother. So ashamed were they of what they had done that they set out across the world to try to forget their sin. They had one strange adventure after another. They came to a land where fire burned everywhere; they met trolls with claws like seals'; and for a while they lived with the bottomless ones— people who had no bottoms and who ate only to belch up their food because it could not pass through them. At last the brother and the sister fell in love with each other and longed to be born again into a new life. At first they thought of being turned into animals of some kind, but they could not agree on a kind that pleased them both. Then the sister said: "Why don't we be something else? Why don't we be the Sun and the Moon?" The boy said nothing. The girl, when she got no answer, did not give up. She ran into the snow house for fire and lighted a torch of moss. The boy, seeing what his sister did, did the same. They came out of the snow house together and ran around it, waving their torches in wide circles—the girl in front and the boy behind. Suddenly they felt themselves lifted from the ground and floated up high into the air. Then the sister put out her brother's torch, but kept her own lighted. They drifted up to the top of the sky, and there the sister, because her torch still burned, turned into the Sun and gave warmth to the earth. The brother, because his torch was out, turned into the Moon, which is just as cold today as it was in the beginning.

The same fanciful touch ran through the Kikerktarmiut's dreams about the world to come. The stars were "the lighted windows of the villages of the dead." There were two happy places to go after death—one up in the sky and the other down in the earth. In both places the hunting was good and there was plenty of time for play. To these two places went the skillful hunters and the women with beautiful tattooing, for they were the ones who were pleasing to the ruling spirits. Somewhere in between, just under the surface of the earth, there was a third place for men too lazy to hunt and for women not willing to suffer tattooing in order to pretty themselves. They had no more energy after death than in life. All day long they sat on their heels, their heads hung down until their chins rested on their chests, and their eyes half closed in a sort of torpor. They were always hungry, but all they had to eat was butterflies. When one of these flew over, they slowly raised their heads and snapped at it; and as they did, yellow dust flew out from their neckbands.

By the end of August the countryside began to take on a wintry look. The smaller lakes skimmed over with ice, and there were cold winds and snow flurries. What we call autumn was for these people the beginning of winter. Soon the caribou would be moving south to the continent; again the hunt for food and clothing must begin. With the autumn hunt in mind the Kikerktarmiut left Amitsoq and trekked southward to Simpson Strait. At its narrowest point the caribou crossed in autumn from the island to the mainland,

and the Eskimos waited for them at Malerualik—the place where one follows the caribou.

With the first heavy snowfalls in September and the freezing of the larger lakes, the caribou gathered in small herds on the island and started for Simpson Strait. All the way down across the island the small herds merged into bigger ones, until the animals were traveling in great droves. At last they came to the shore near Malerualik, where they poured down over the ridges to the sea, their hoofs clattering and their heads held high. But the Kikerktarmiut were already there in hiding; as the caribou hesitated before crossing, the arrows began to fly and the first animals fell. More herds were to come and more caribou to be killed, until at last the natives had enough for food and clothing. Then the hunting was over. There followed a time of making meat caches, preparing skins and sewing new, warm clothes. After that the Island Dwellers went out on the ice again to seal; one round of seasons had come to its end, another round had begun.

Year after year this life went on unchanged, lived by a handful of people who could seldom number themselves above a hundred and fifty, as if a magic spell had been cast over them —a spell which no one from another world had yet come to break. Meanwhile their island continued its rise from the sea; by the beginning of the nineteenth century, it spread over an area of nearly 4,800 square miles and at its nearest point was but three miles from the continental shore.

By the beginning of that century, too, explorers, searching for a northwest passage, began to push their way toward the island through the channels of the Arctic Archipelago. Other explorers, bent on charting the arctic coast of North America, were bound sooner or later to find the island. As it turned out, the first party of white men to discover Kikerktak came from the east, from a ship icebound off the shore of Boothia. The second party came from the south, down a great river that empties into the Polar Sea near Kikerktak. The third, in two sea boats, came along the continental coast from the west— from the mouth of the Coppermine. Then from the north in two ships came a fourth party to meet tragedy on the shores of Kikerktak and to give to the island a role in history far above that of any other arctic island in the world.

PART II
The Island Is Discovered

1.

On both sides of Kikerktak stretches the arctic coast of North America. By 1800 only three expeditions had visited this coast. Samuel Hearne, in 1771, had reached the mouth of the Coppermine River overland, searching on behalf of the Hudson's Bay Company for copper reported by Indians. Seven years later Captain James Cook had sailed through Bering Strait and traced the continental coast to Icy Cape, in longitude 161° 42′ west—one hundred and fifty miles short of Point Barrow. Alexander Mackenzie, in the summer of 1789, had descended from Great Slave Lake to the mouth of the river that now bears his name. In other words, with the exception of where the Coppermine and the Mackenzie entered the Polar Sea, there lay between Icy Cape and Repulse Bay—the northernmost inlet of Hudson Bay—some 3,000 miles of coast as a ship would sail, all of it north of the Arctic Circle and none of it yet touched by explorers; it was still the object of their dreams.

Much the same can be said of the Arctic Archipelago, of which Kikerktak was a part: it, too, north of the Circle, was almost completely unexplored. John Davis, on his first voyage from England (1585) in quest of the Northwest Passage, had sighted the eastern coast of Baffin Land, the long island that caps Hudson Bay on the north, in latitude 66° 40′ north. Just south of that latitude, in Exeter Sound, he anchored his two tiny barks, the 50-ton *Sunshine* and the 35-ton *Moonshine*, "in a very faire rode, under a very brave mount, the cliffes whereof were as orient as gold." The road he named Totnes Road and the mount, Mount Raleigh. He found the country strange and wonderful, with willows growing like shrubs and flowers that reminded him of primroses. A raven was seen on Mount Raleigh, and at the mountain's foot four bears. The hunt that followed is best described in the words of a member of the party:

> So soone as we were come to anker in Totnes Rode under Mt. Raleigh, we espied 4 white beares at the foote of the mount. We supposing them to bee goates or wolves, manned our boats, and went towards them: but when wee came neere the shore, wee found them to be white beares of a monstrous bignesse: we being desirous of fresh victual and the sport, began to assault them, and I being on land one of them came down the hil right against me; my piece was charged with haileshot and a bullet, I discharged my piece and shot him in the necke: hee roared a litle and tooke the water straight, making smal account of his hurt. Then we followed him in our boate, and killed him with boare speares, and two more that night. We found nothing in their mawes, but we judged by their dung, that they fed upon grasse, because it appeared in al respects like the dung of an horse, wherein we might very plainely see the very strawes.

On his next two voyages (1586 and 1587) Davis again saw Mount Raleigh—on the last voyage from the deck of a 20-ton pinnace, in which he had first sailed up the west coast of Greenland as far as Sanderson's Hope, the lofty headland near

Upernavik, and then, by skirting the southern edge of the vast mass of ice floes that drifts down Baffin Bay, had crossed over to Baffin Land and a familiar coast.

In 1616 William Baffin, in one of the boldest adventures of all time, sailed the 55-ton *Discovery*—the same ship Hudson had used in his exploration of Hudson Bay in 1610—up past Sanderson's Hope to the top of the great bay that lies above Davis Strait. There he discovered and named Smith Sound, the beginning of the narrow waters that separate Greenland and Ellesmere Island. On his way back, down the western side of Baffin Bay, he stopped at Jones Sound, at the southern end of Ellesmere. There a boat was sent ashore for a brief visit. Farther south, still hugging the shore of the archipelago, he sighted Lancaster Sound, broad and running deep to the west; a ledge of ice blocked the entrance to it. Though Baffin gave the name "Sound" to all three of the openings he sighted, he thought of them rather as bays, and he returned home convinced that north of Davis Strait there was no passage or hope of a passage to the Orient.

Two hundred years passed, and no explorer followed in Baffin's track. At long last, in the year 1818, the British Admiralty sent out a new expedition "to seek a Northern Passage, by Sea, from the Atlantic to the Pacific Ocean." In command was Captain John Ross, an experienced naval officer who had seen service in the Baltic and the White Sea and had three times been wounded in action. Ross did no better than Baffin. To him, too, Smith Sound and Jones Sound were nothing but bays, and at Lancaster Sound he thought he saw a continuous mountain range closing the end of the Sound. He named the distant range the Croker Mountains, after the Secretary of the Admiralty. He confirmed the correctness of

Baffin's latitudes, but he saw no possibility of getting farther west.

In Ross's party, second in command, was Lieutenant Edward Parry, a daring young naval officer who, at twenty-eight, had already seen fifteen years of service and been in many actions, one of them in America in the War of 1812. Parry returned to England from the Ross expedition not at all convinced that a range of mountains shut off Lancaster Sound. In his opinion Ross had missed the chance of a great discovery: down Lancaster Sound, Parry was certain, lay the long dreamed of Northwest Passage. The next year he set sail to prove his point. In command of two ships, the *Hecla* and the *Griper*, he entered Lancaster Sound on August 4. At the western end of the Sound, he turned into Prince Regent Inlet and explored it south for one hundred and twenty miles. He then returned to Lancaster Sound and sailed westward down a broad and long avenue of waterways to the far side of the archipelago. As he went, he named the islands that he passed: to starboard, North Devon, Cornwallis, Bathurst and Melville; on his port side, North Somerset, Prince of Wales and Banks. On September 17 he reached McClure Strait, the western exit of the middle passage through the archipelago; the exit was blocked by ice heavier than any he had ever seen. He knew it would be disastrous for a ship to be trapped in such ice; despite this, for a week he tried to push his way through. In the end he had to give up and winter at Winter Harbour on the southeastern coast of Melville Island. The next summer he tried the same route again; again the ice blocked him. In the autumn he returned to England.

Parry had done what no one would ever do again: in a single season, by sail alone, he had gone from one side of the archipelago to the other. He was now more certain than ever that he could find a way to the Pacific but it would have to lie farther south—nearer the continent and the yet-undiscovered Kikerktak. It would have to be far enough south to bypass the heavy pack ice that poured into McClure Strait from the western sea. In May, 1821, he sailed from England again, his way this time through Hudson Strait and up into Foxe Basin north of Hudson Bay to see what luck lay there. At the northern end of Foxe Basin he discovered, leading westward, a strait that he named Fury and Hecla, after his two ships; at the strait's western end, which he reached on foot, he stood but two hundred and fifty miles from Kikerktak. Because of ice he never succeeded in getting his ships through. After two winters in the pack he returned home, unsuccessful but not discouraged. He was of the opinion that Fury and Hecla Strait led into a sea that could be reached by sailing down Prince Regent Inlet, and that out of this sea might lead a passage to the west.

In 1824 he sailed to seek this passage; once more with the *Fury* and the *Hecla* he headed for the Arctic Archipelago. The season was a late one, and the ice of Baffin Bay unusually close-packed. He was held up forty days battling his way across the bay to Lancaster Sound; it was September before he reached Prince Regent Inlet. There freeze-up overtook him, and he went into winter quarters at Port Bowen, seventy-five miles down the inlet's eastern shore.

The ships were not released from the ice until the next July, when they stood over to the west side of the inlet to shape a southern course. There drifting ice caught them and pushed them ashore. The *Hecla* was got off, but not the *Fury*, which had been badly damaged by the ice. An effort was made to lighten her by dumping her provisions and stores ashore. Even so relieved, the ship could not be floated, and there was no choice but to abandon her where she lay—seventy miles north of a possible passage to the west and to Kikerktak. The site of the disaster became known as Fury Beach. The *Fury*'s crew boarded the *Hecla* and took with them what supplies would be needed on the way home; the rest—coal, salt meat, lime juice, canisters of preserved meats and vegetables, sugar, and similar supplies and provisions—were piled high on the shore in tents and in the open, a boon to any later expedition that came that way. With the abandonment of the *Fury* Parry's adventures in the northern archipelago came to an end. His first voyage had been successful beyond all dreams, his last one so great a failure as to discourage the Admiralty for the time being from further attempts at exploration among the islands and waterways north of the American continent.

During the years when Parry was searching among the islands of the archipelago for a way to Bering Strait, two expeditions had set out from England for Canada to go north across that vast country and survey parts of the arctic coast. They, too, were working on the problem of a Northwest Passage; the tracing of the arctic coast would afford—though perhaps only by shallow, offshore waters—a route from the Atlantic to the Pacific around the top of North America. In command of the two land expeditions was John Franklin, a British naval officer with a dream of being an arctic explorer and a flair for adventure. In 1800, at the age of fourteen, he had entered the British Royal Navy and just after his fifteenth birthday had taken part under Nelson in the destruction of the Danish fleet at Copenhagen. Next, under his cousin, Captain Matthew Flinders, he spent two years surveying the coast of Australia; on his way home, he was shipwrecked on a reef off the coast of Queensland. At nineteen, in 1805, again under Nelson, he saw the destruction of the French and Spanish fleets at Trafalgar; nine years later, he was wounded at the battle of New Orleans.

In 1818—a year before setting out for the Canadian Northwest—Franklin had his first arctic experience. That year the Admiralty sent two ships, the *Dorothea* and the *Trent*, to sail to Spitsbergen and from there to cross the polar seas, as far north as the North Pole if necessary, to Bering Strait and Hawaii. The Admiralty was acting on a belief that a great unfrozen sea, fringed by a barrier of ice, covered the top of the world; once access to this sea had been gained, there would be free sailing from one side to the other. It was on this dream expedition that Franklin, second in command and master of the *Trent*, set sail. With him, as midshipman, he had a twenty-one-year-old named George Back, also a seeker after high adventure and rough going, a young man to whom the Arctic became an everlasting and fascinating challenge.

If risk and hardship were what these two men wanted, they got their hearts' desire, and in full measure, before their first arctic voyage was over. For thirteen days their ship was beset in the pack north of Spitsbergen and so relentlessly squeezed that she opened at every seam. At one time the ice piled up above the bulwarks, and the ship was twisted until "the doors of all the cabins flew open, and the panels of some started in the frames, while her false stern-port was moved three inches and her timbers cracked to a most serious extent." A gale then came up, and the pounding floes battered the ship nearly to pieces. The *Trent* and her consort, the *Dorothea*, were compelled to seek refuge in Fairhaven Harbor on the coast of

33

Spitsbergen, where it took a month to put the two ships in shape for the return voyage to England. As a voyage to the top of the world the expedition was a flat failure, its farthest north having been no more than 80° 34'. Far from satisfying Franklin's and Back's appetites for adventure, it had served only to whet them; thereafter neither man could rest until he had returned to the North time and time again.

It was in the year following this adventure, 1819, that Lieutenant Franklin set forth to survey the arctic coast of North America. With him were George Back and another midshipman, Robert Hood; a Royal Navy surgeon, Doctor Richardson, who was also a naturalist; and a bluejacket named Hepburn. With help from the Hudson's Bay Company the party was to descend the Coppermine River and survey the coast eastward from the Coppermine's mouth. The party reached York Factory, above James Bay on the west side of Hudson Bay, in August. Proceeding from York by the fur traders' route to the northwest, they stopped at Norway House at the northern end of Lake Winnipeg and at Cumberland House, one hundred and eighty miles from Norway House, on the Saskatchewan. Early in the winter of 1820 they reached Fort Chipewyan at the western end of Lake Athabasca, and on July 15 they were at Fort Providence at the western end of Great Slave Lake. Here the party was augmented by voyageurs and native hunters and guides. On August 2 the party was off for the mouth of the Yellowknife River, or, as it was known to the Indians, the Begholodessy, the River of the Toothless Fish. This river pours into North Arm, the most northerly extension of Great Slave Lake. On August 3 the expedition reached the Yellowknife, and nine days later, after a journey of one hundred and fifty-six miles, was at the river's source. By a chain of lakes they continued north some thirty miles farther to Winter Lake, reported to be near the headwaters of the Coppermine. A fine stand of pines being available, they set themselves to the work of building suitable winter quarters, appropriately named Fort Enterprise. They were now in unexplored territory; conditions were unfamiliar; for much of their food they were dependent on an Indian chief named Akaitcho and his hunters.

The next summer, in July, Franklin, with his four English companions and the voyageurs, hunters and guides, started down the Coppermine River. Before leaving Fort Enterprise, Franklin exacted from Akaitcho a promise to provision the fort against the possibility of the party's return in the fall. Traveling first across the frozen lakes with sledges, then down the river in canoes, Franklin's party reached the Coppermine's mouth and the Arctic Sea on July 18.

On July 21 the coastal party, twenty strong, started eastward along the coast in two birch bark canoes. The voyage was perilous; ice threatened to smash the fragile canoes and waves to swamp them. The coast did not trend unbrokenly eastward, as Franklin had hoped. The party spent from July 25 to August 16 exploring the long southern reach of Bathurst Inlet. By the time they arrived at the western tip of Kent Peninsula food was short, the boats were badly broken, and the men were grumbling openly, even in the presence of the officers. Still Franklin persisted in his object of exploring the continent's northern coast, and by August 18, against fearful natural odds, he had reached Point Turnagain on Kent Peninsula, about six and a half degrees east of the mouth of the Coppermine and only two hundred and fifty miles from the nearest point of Kikerktak.

Cold weather was setting in; provisions had run low; plans for the return to Fort Enterprise had to be made. With the canoes battered and broken, it seemed folly to go back over their sea route to the mouth of the Coppermine, particularly as the season of gales would soon be on them. Instead they sailed back to Bathurst Inlet and crossed it to Arctic Sound and from there ascended the Hood River—so named by Franklin on the outward voyage. On September 3 they struck off from the Hood directly across the Barren Lands to Fort Enterprise, one hundred and fifty miles away.

The adventure quickly turned into tragedy. For a few days after leaving the Hood, the hunters were able to get fresh meat, but the deeper they penetrated into the Barren Lands, the more meager became the supply of game. Soon the only fresh food was an occasional ptarmigan; once the men fed on the remains of a caribou that had been killed and three-quarters eaten by wolves. Pemmican and concentrated soups gave out; the men tried to live on tripe-de-roche, a bitter and barely life-sustaining lichen that brought on diarrhea.

The party weakened fast and pitiably. Their fishing nets became too heavy to carry; they left them behind and burned the floats for fuel. Two portable canoes that had been fashioned out of the big ones were abandoned; the men were too weak to carry them. Now no rivers could be crossed except on improvised rafts; because the men had to walk around the innumerable lakes that break the Barren Lands, their journey was lengthened by endless miles. Cold weather came, and snow and winter wind; still the men struggled on in their misery.

On September 26, they reached the Coppermine River, forty miles north of Fort Enterprise. In a tiny, makeshift canoe, improvised from willow splints and canvas, they ferried the Coppermine one by one. Back, with four men, immediately set out for Fort Enterprise to get provisions and Indian help. On October 11, Franklin and four others reached the fort; they had had to leave behind Hood, Richardson, Hepburn, and the few other men still surviving. Franklin found the fort empty of provisions; Akaitcho had failed to supply it for the returning party. A note from Back said that he had gone in search of help and would proceed to Fort Providence if necessary. On October 29, Richardson and Hepburn came into the fort with a sickening tale of cannibalism and of the murder of Hood.

The party at the fort faced slow starvation; for food they had nothing but charred bones and bits of burned caribou skin picked from the ashes of former fires. Two of the natives died; the rest of the party were near death when help arrived. Back, on his journey, had come upon Indians whom he sent to the men at Enterprise. With food and care, the survivors were nursed back to health. By the end of November they were able to travel, and on December 18 they were at Fort Resolution. There Back was waiting for them. The Englishmen wintered at the fort and in late May began the long overland journey to York Factory. In October they were in England. They had been gone three and a half years, and by land and water had made a journey in the new world of North America of more than 5,200 miles.

For most persons the experience of the march across the Barren Lands would have finished off any lure the North might have had; it had no such effect on Franklin and Back and Richardson. In July 1826, with the faithful Hepburn, and with Kendall, an officer in Parry's last expedition, filling in for the murdered Hood, they were on the arctic coast again, this time at the mouth of the Mackenzie, and traveling not in canoes but in four stout sea boats, one twenty-six feet long. At the outlet of the Mackenzie the party split: Franklin and Back to survey the coast westward, if possible as far as Icy Cape; and Richardson and Kendall to go eastward to the mouth of the Coppermine, thus connecting their survey with Franklin's previous exploration of the coast. Richardson and Kendall reached their goal; Franklin and Back were less successful. They surveyed three hundred and seventy-four miles of new coast, their farthest point Return Reef, one hundred and fifty miles east of Point Barrow. The going was hard all the way, with heavy fogs and close-packed ice. At Return Reef they waited six days for conditions to improve, in the hope that they would be able to push on; but there was no change. The middle of August had passed; Franklin reluctantly turned back. He knew, of course, that Captain Frederick William Beechey, a former shipmate on the *Trent*, had been sent in the ship *Blossom* around South America to Bering Strait, to meet Franklin at the western end of the Northwest Passage. Franklin learned only later that the *Blossom* had reached Icy Cape, and that from Icy Cape, during the August days when Franklin was waiting and trying to push westward from Return Reef, a boat party from the *Blossom* was heading for Point Barrow.

Slowly the explorer was penetrating the Arctic Archipelago, slowly he was working his way along the northern coast of the continent; Kikerktak could not escape discovery for long.

2.

Ten years after John Ross mistook Lancaster Sound for a bay, he was again ready to be off for the North. During the ten years, he had submitted a scheme for further northern exploration to the Admiralty, but it had not met with their approval. Not to be denied, he had turned for financial help to a rich friend and benefactor, Felix Booth, distiller and Sheriff of London.

Ross's plan was to pick up the trail of the Northwest Passage at Fury Beach, the farthest reach of Parry's third expedition to the archipelago. From Fury Beach he would sail down Prince Regent Inlet to seek a passage to the west. Bellot Strait was still undiscovered; with luck, Ross might happen on it and sail through and reach the shores of Kikerktak. For his voyage he had purchased at Liverpool the *Victory*, an 85-tonner, which had once been used as a packet on the run between Liverpool and the Isle of Man. The *Victory* was a three-master with paddle wheels, and the honor of first using steam in the North was to be hers. Steam promised much for northern travel, especially in calm waters and in the leads among the ice floes. There, where sails were often useless, the *Victory* should be able to plug along at a reasonable speed under her own power. Her original paddles had been replaced by new-fangled ones that could be lifted from the water at a moment's notice. Her high pressure engine and the boilers and bellows (there was no flue) were not altogether a convenience; they took up so much room as to leave not enough for all the provisions and supplies. The overflow was loaded aboard a decked sloop, the 16-ton *Krusenstern*, which was towed out behind.

The *Victory* carried four officers and nineteen men, among them several with previous arctic experience. A nephew of Captain Ross's, James Clark Ross, age twenty-nine, was second in command. He had been aboard the *Isabella* with his uncle in 1818 and on four voyages with Parry—three to the archipelago and one toward the Pole. William Thom, purser, had also been on John Ross's first expedition. Thomas Blanky, first mate, had twice visited the North, and Thomas Aber-nethy, second mate, had been aboard the *Fury* when she was wrecked in Prince Regent Inlet.

The *Victory* sailed from Woolwich, on the Thames, on May 23, 1829. She rounded the southern coast of England and headed up through the Irish Sea. Hardly was she out of sight of land when the engine developed piston trouble and the boilers began to leak. A week out from Woolwich Captain Ross, exasperated, wrote in his journal: "Even with a pressure of forty-five pounds on the inch, we could never obtain more than fifteen strokes in the minute; and as it thence followed, that the outer edge of the paddles had no greater velocity than five miles in the hour, that of the vessel could not possibly exceed three. The boilers also continued to leak, though we had put dung and potatoes in them, by Mr. Erickson's direction." Not many days later the boilers burst, and at

Port Logan, near the entrance to the North Channel, one of the smaller boilers was put ashore. In the channel other troubles plagued the ship and her master. A gale broke the head of the foremast; a shortage of hay and water compelled them to kill one of two precious bullocks that had been taken along to be slaughtered and frozen at the edge of the ice.

Out in the Atlantic things took a turn for the better. With fair weather and favorable winds the expedition made the crossing to Cape Farewell, the southernmost point of Greenland, in ten days; they sighted the cape at a distance of thirty-one leagues on the evening of July 1. That same day warm clothing was issued—to each man "a blue jacket and trousers, a flannel shirt, a comfortable, a pair of wadmal hose, a pair of flannel drawers, a Welsh wig, a pair of sea boots, and another of carpet boots." On July 12 they entered Davis Strait, and the next day they had the excitement of seeing their first iceberg.

Their progress north in Davis Strait was slow. The weather was calm or the winds contrary, and for ten days they beat aimlessly about. They had engine trouble and more engine trouble; the boilers continued to leak, one so badly it had to be disconnected; the ship's speed under full steam was automatically reduced to one and a half miles an hour. By July 23 the *Victory* had crossed the Arctic Circle and was at the Danish settlement of Holsteinborg. From there on the going improved. They reached their farthest north, 74° 14', six days after leaving Holsteinborg and crossed to the west side of Baffin Bay through an almost iceless sea, with the weather so warm that the men scrubbed the decks in bare feet. On August 6 they entered Lancaster Sound. Three days later, in the Sound, ". . . no ice of any kind was in sight; but the snowy tops of the mountains, and particularly of the two remarkable ones formerly named Catharine and Elizabeth, were seen rising above the clouds." Slowly the *Victory* sailed into the solitude and bleak beauty of the North.

At Fury Beach the party found everything Parry had unloaded from his ship much as he had left it four years before. Of the *Fury* herself there was not a sign; apparently the ice had carried her away. One tent still stood on the beach; bears had pulled down the others. The canisters of preserved meats and vegetables lay piled in two heaps, untouched. The contents were not frozen and still tasted good. The wine, spirits, sugar, flour and cocoa had not spoiled at all; the lime juice and pickles a little, but not much. Ross's men took aboard the *Victory* sufficient provisions and supplies, including ten tons of coal, to complete the *Victory's* equipment for two and a half years; twenty-four hours after landing they were on their way again.

They soon passed Cape Garry, which marked the extremity of the explored coast; through an ice-filled sea they headed into the unknown. At Brentford Bay they missed their one chance of finding a passage to the west—Bellot Strait. In the same bay the magnetic needle showed a dip of 89°; they saw many whales, and the churning of the paddles roused up seals in great numbers. Slowly still, they quested southward, down a coast broken and hollowed into little bays and skirted by rocks and islands. To the west, beyond the low shore, rose a range of granite hills, blue in the northern haze. Ross called the land Boothia Felix, and to every new island of any size and to every bay and every headland he gave a name. Christening new lands in all their parts was, after all, the explorer's privilege, and part of the fun of the game. Ross and his officers and men made side trips ashore and found abandoned Eskimo encampments and plants in flower and the bones of foxes and the teeth of musk oxen. In the excitement of making new discoveries the slowness of their progress southward was forgotten. By the end of August, two weeks after leaving Cape Garry, they had sailed past only a little over a hundred miles of new coast.

With September the weather grew colder and the gales more frequent. Drifting ice filled the channels between the shore and the off-lying islands, and snow began to show on the hill tops. Ice so hemmed in the ship the first day of the month that Ross feared she was being permanently beset; but on the fifth day she was released, and ship and crew were on their way again. As the early winter of the high latitudes advanced, delays were more and more frequent, the going harder. Still they pressed forward down the desolate coast, until at last they came to where it turned westward into Lord Mayor Bay. A little beyond this point, across the mouth of Thom Bay, ice stopped all further progress, and the *Victory* went into winter quarters at Felix Harbour on the eastern side of the narrow isthmus that connects Boothia with the mainland, hardly 125 miles from the nearest point of Kikerktak.

The *Victory*'s run, for a single season in the North, had been a good one. Ross's dream of a passage to the west had not, of course, been fulfilled, but he had not lost hope of finding the route he sought. Now it was important to make the ship as snug as possible for the winter months ahead. Already freeze-up was well on the way, and the ground was white with snow. First the crew dismantled the engine and put it ashore; it had been nothing but a disappointment, and with its running gear and tools it took up two-thirds of the ship's tonnage—space badly needed during a wintering. Next, rigging and sails were taken down and the deck housed over with canvas. The carpenters then altered the cabin to make it warmer. After alterations, the temperature of the cabin mounted to a steady 45°; before, its highest had been 28°. Ross's own words best describe scenes aboard and what the ship looked like when winter routine was established.

The men slept in hammocks, which were taken down at six in the morning, and hung up at ten at night, being also aired twice a week. The lower deck, being the dwelling floor, was covered with hot sand every morning, and scrubbed with sand till eight, when the men breakfasted. Monday was settled in future as the washing day; and this operation being finished by noon, the linen was dried at the stove. The upper deck having been at length covered with snow two feet and a half in thickness, it was trod down till it became a solid mass of ice, and was then sprinkled with sand, so as to put on the appearance of a rolled gravel walk. Above this, was the roof already mentioned, of which the canvas sides were continued so low as to cover those of the ship. The surrounding bank of snow, being completed, reached to the ship's gunwale, so that the union of this with the roof formed a perfect shelter from all wind, and thus excluded, very materially, the impressions of the external cold. In the same manner there was a covering of snow to the cabin deck, while the skylight was fitted with double sashes: but the way from the cabin to the deck was not closed, since the frost was not yet so intense as to render that necessary: the inner doors were merely fitted with ropes and pulleys.

Inside this seeming fortress of snow, life went on at a strictly regulated pace. Breakfast, at eight, consisted of tea and cocoa; for noon dinner, there were tinned meats or salt beef or pork with rice, dumplings, or a similar starch. If the weather permitted, the men then worked outside the ship until four. When the weather was bad, the men walked a certain number of hours on deck, under the roofing. The last meal of the day, usually bread and tea, was served at five; from six to nine, an evening school was held. Then the hammocks were slung, and the men were in bed by ten. Little wonder that a northern winter was looked forward to with a certain amount of gloom.

Christmas came, heralded by an unusually brilliant display of northern lights. The restriction on grog was lifted. For dinner all hands ate roast beef and potatoes and mince pie and iced cherry brandy with its fruit. And in the afternoon sky Venus shone, brighter and clearer than they had ever before seen it. With the New Year the weather settled in cold; at noontime the sky glowed with red and purple tints. On January 9 the first Eskimos appeared; thirty-one in all, they were members of a community camped only a short distance from the ship. They provided an endless diversion for the men and officers of the *Victory*. The ship's carpenter made a wooden leg for one Eskimo who had lost his own limb to a polar bear. Bartering was carried on at a fine pace, and there was frequent visiting back and forth between the ship and the snow house village.

Most important, these Eskimos knew the geography of the region. From them James Clark Ross learned that to the west, across the narrow isthmus, lay a great sea. Also, they told him —although they had the information by hearsay only—there was a water passage to this sea at a place called Awwuktoo-teak (the little place where whales abound). They were right about a passage—Bellot Strait; they were wrong about its location, which they put at only seventy miles—just half the actual distance—north of Felix Harbour. On February 9 the temperature fell to $-47°$, and ten days later they had the first snowfall of the new year. The Eskimos supplied the Englishmen with seal meat and other game; they brought warm clothing and skins, which they bartered for next to nothing; their friendliness was beyond belief.

The party's impatience for spring grew as the hours of daylight lengthened. The Eskimos' information about a sea to the west and a passage to this sea by the north suggested that great discoveries might lie close at hand. Early in April James Clark Ross set out on a sledge journey across the Isthmus of Boothia to the head of Spence Bay. There, from his Eskimo guide Ooblooria, he learned that beyond Spence Bay, to the north, the west, and the south, stretched a sea that was free of all ice during the summer. The *Victory* could reach this sea by sailing first north, then west through the passage at Awwuktooteak; but there was no passage to it from any point south of where the *Victory* lay. Ross took Ooblooria to mean that there was no way into the sea at all from the south—no Rae Strait or Simpson Strait as we know them today. He believed he was standing on the side of a great gulf of the western sea—a gulf bounded on the south by the continental shore. With this understanding Ross returned to the ship; later in the month, with the Eskimo Pooyetta, he journeyed the seventy miles north to Awwuktooteak to seek the strait there —only to find nothing but a bay. This convinced him that the Eskimo story of a passage to the west had no basis in fact and that in all probability the coast of Boothia Felix stretched unbroken right up to Barrow Strait.

If, then, the *Victory* could not be got around to the western sea, should not the coast of that sea be explored on foot? Perhaps Franklin's Point Turnagain could be reached and all

46

the coastline between it and Boothia explored. With this possibility in mind, James Clark Ross and three companions left
the ship on May 17 and headed westward. They crossed the
Isthmus of Boothia, continued west along the northern edge
of Spence Bay, then turned up the west coast of Boothia and
followed it into Josephine Bay. From there, at Cape Cambridge, the western headland of Josephine Bay, he cut across
the sea to Matty Island, then on to Kikerktak. The first white
man had arrived from the east.

Ross started to follow the coast north. The party traveled
at night, to avoid the risk of snow blindness; during the day
they slept in burrows in the snow. The going was hard; some
of the dogs sickened and died; the thick fog froze to the men's
clothing, making it almost impossible to move. Ross shot two
ptarmigan, "which not only gave us what was now rare, a
warm meal, but enabled us to save our provisions." He saw
several stone huts, which looked as if they had been occupied
by natives not long before. But not one of the Kikerktarmiut
did he meet; there was no one to tell him that what he was on
was not the mainland at all but an island.

At midnight on May 28 Ross reached Cape Felix. "Here,"
he wrote, "we found the land trend to the south-west, while
the vast extent of ocean then before our eyes, assured us that
we had at length reached the northern point of that portion
of the continent which I had already ascertained with so
much satisfaction to be trending toward Cape Turnagain.
The pack of ice which had, in the autumn of the last year,
been pressed against that shore, consisted of the heaviest
masses that I had ever seen in such a situation. With this, the
lighter floes had been thrown up, on some parts of the coast,
in a most extraordinary and incredible manner; turning up

large quantities of the shingle before them, and, in some places, having travelled as much as half a mile beyond the limits of the highest tide-mark." Ross had no doubt that he was standing on one of the great northern capes of the continent and that to the southwest the coast ran unbroken to Franklin's Point Turnagain.

The party pushed on six hours beyond Cape Felix before making camp. They had now been thirteen days on the way; more than half of their twenty-one days' provisions were used up. Any idea of getting to Point Turnagain, 250 miles away as the crow flies, had to be abandoned. The most they could grant themselves was an advance of a few more hours, and that, for the sake of speed, with a small and lightly loaded party. The two members with the sorest feet were detailed to keep camp; and at eight o'clock in the evening of May 29 Ross and Abernethy pushed ahead down the coast.

Four hours later, at midnight, they halted their march on a low, flat point of land, to which they gave the name of their ship—Victory. A mass of ice forty feet high lay stranded on the beach. From the top of it Ross gazed southwestward along what he thought was continental shore. He named the farthest point of land in sight Cape Franklin and a nearer point Cape Jane Franklin, after the renowned explorer and his wife. He and Abernethy then built on Victory Point a stone cairn six feet high and placed in it a canister containing a record of the expedition's accomplishments. At one o'clock of the 30th they began their journey back to their companions at the camp; on the way they found a piece of driftwood and had the good luck to shoot a hare and two ptarmigan.

The next day the entire party set out for the ship, not as they had come, by way of Cape Felix, but straight across the

island to Cape Sidney on its eastern side. South of Cape
Sidney they saw many circles of tent stones where the Kikerktarmiut had camped, and they bagged two ptarmigan and a
fox. They followed down the east coast until they were opposite the southern tip of Matty Island, when they cut across
the ice to Spence Bay. On the ice between Kikerktak and
Boothia, Ross looked southward through a thin haze and
thought he saw the continental shore, and later dotted it in on
his chart as such. The glimpse of land to the south confirmed
his belief that there was a continuous coastline between
Boothia and Cape Felix and Victory Point, and to this new
region he gave the name of King William Land. To those
discoverers who came after him his chart would show the
sea on the east side of Kikerktak—the sea that, as Ooblo-
ria said, was free of all ice during the summer—as a dead end,
with no way out of it to the south. It was a mistake that others
would pay for with their lives. On June 13 Ross and his party,
after an absence of a little under a month, were once again back
at the ship.

The summer that followed was an anxious one; it seemed
that the ice would never break up and free the ship. A party
journeyed to the head of Thom Bay and purchased a great
supply of fish from the natives—a ton of salmon in exchange
for a knife. What surprised the Englishmen more than the
bargain price was the natives' ravenous appetite. At one meal,
while five Englishmen ate a total of a salmon and a half, or
an average of two pounds apiece, each Eskimo devoured two
seven-pound fish and apparently thought nothing of it. The
men got the *Victory* ready for sea and waited to be off. July
and August passed; still the ice held the ship fast. Not until
two o'clock on the afternoon of September 17 was the vessel

free and under sail again, and then the reward of so much waiting was a poor one: soon the wind and the ice forced the *Victory* to seek shelter in Sheriff Harbour, only three miles up the coast north of Felix Harbour. There she was soon imprisoned, with no release possible until summer should come again. The second winter went by much as the one before; it was more boring; a good deal of the novelty of the North had worn off.

When James Clark Ross left England, it was commonly supposed that the North Magnetic Pole lay at 70° of north latitude and 98° 30′ of west longitude. If this were so, Ross, when at Cape Felix, had been within ten miles of its position. At the time he did not have with him the proper instruments for exactly locating the pole; he came back to the *Victory* disappointed at having been so near the magic spot and yet so unable to prove its precise position. During the *Victory*'s second winter, however, Ross concluded from the most painstaking observations that the Magnetic Pole was not on King William Land at all, but somewhere on the west coast of Boothia north of Cape Cambridge. As soon as spring came and sledding was possible, he set out to find it.

Who has not wondered about this mysterious spot? Who has not imagined it to be a great mountain of metal or a huge buried magnet of some kind? What else could account for its drawing power? The thought of it takes us back to our childhood, and again we are magnetizing a needle and then floating the needle, with the help of vaseline, on the surface of the water in the wash basin. Slowly the needle swings this way and that way, and finally settles for the north. Then, for an enchanted instant, we know that the world is as marvelous a place as we have always believed it to be.

It must have been just such a sense of wonder that stirred
James Clark Ross and made him seek his goal. On May 19,
he and his party, in company with a second party under his
uncle, left the ship and crossed the isthmus by an upper route,
through a chain of lakes that took them directly from the
southwest corner of Thom Bay across to Josephine Bay,
which they reached a week later. On the way they met a
group of traveling Eskimos who had a sledge made all of ice,
very delicate in appearance and as beautiful as if wrought
from crystal. At Josephine Bay, on the 27th, the two parties
separated: John Ross to explore the coast to the eastward, his
nephew to the westward. The latter, with his party, rounded
Cape Cambridge and continued northward. On May 31, at
eight o'clock in the morning, their instruments showed them
that the magnetic pole was fourteen miles away; twenty-four
hours later they had reached their goal. Except for the spots
effect on the compass and the dipping needle, there was nothing to distinguish it from the rest of the countryside. As Ross
described it:

> The land at this place is very low near the coast, but it rises
> into ridges of fifty or sixty feet high about a mile inland. We
> could have wished that a place so important had possessed
> more of mark or note. It was scarcely censurable to regret
> that there was not a mountain to indicate a spot to which so
> much of interest must ever be attached; and I could even
> have pardoned any one among us who had been so romantic
> or absurd as to expect that the magnetic pole was an object
> as conspicuous and mysterious as the fabled mountain of
> Sinbad, that it even was a mountain of iron, or a magnet as
> large as Mont Blanc. But Nature had here erected no monu-
> ment to denote the spot which she had chosen as the centre of
> one of her great and dark powers. . . .

On the spot were some Eskimo snow houses, not long abandoned. Half a mile from these the men made camp; Ross, in one of the snow houses, began his observations. In such a primitive setting exact and scientific knowledge was obtained. Ross saw his dipping needle dip to 89° 59′, or within one minute of the vertical. He saw his horizontal needles, suspended with all care from the ceiling of the snow house, remain motionless: not one swung either to the right or to the left. The magic spot lay underfoot; he was at the focus point of every compass needle in the world. He came out from the house and announced his findings to the men. They fixed the British flag on the spot and took possession in the name of Great Britain and King William the Fourth. They then built a great stone cairn and under it buried a canister with a record of their findings. While the rest of the men waited at the camp, Ross and Abernethy proceeded north for four hours to stretch to the limit their discoveries. At their farthest reach they built a second cairn, and then returned to the rest of the party for the journey home.

The following summer, that of 1831, was passed in the same anxiety as that of the year before. The ice held the ship fast through July, through August. On August 28 the *Victory* broke free and sailed across Thom Bay to Victoria Harbour; there she was beset again. A third winter in the North was more than anyone had bargained for. The monotony was intense; no Eskimos came to trade or to visit. Scurvy afflicted the men, and with scurvy came despondency. For one hundred and thirty-six consecutive days the thermometer never rose above zero. Home seemed far away, and the chances of getting there slim to vanishing. Captain Ross dared not risk his party's waiting another summer to see what the ice would do then; the alternative was to make their way on foot to Fury Beach, there pick up the *Fury's* three boats, and in them continue to Baffin Bay in the hope, thin as it would be, of falling in with a whaler. Ross chose the alternative. During April and May advance depots were laid down along the coast of Boothia north from Victoria Harbour; on May 20 the *Victory's* colors were hoisted and nailed to the mast, and she was abandoned by her officers and men.

A month later the whole party was at Fury Beach. Their first need was shelter, and this they supplied by building a house—Somerset House—thirty-one feet long, sixteen feet wide, and seven feet high, covered with canvas. It had two rooms, one for the men and another, divided into four small cabins, for the officers. By the evening of their first day at Fury Beach the frame was up, and three days later they moved in. The carpenters then set to work to strengthen the mahogany boats, two of which were equipped with leg-of-mutton sails and the third with a spritsail. On August 1 all was in readiness; they had seaworthy boats provisioned for two months and a well-supplied base to fall back on if worse came to worst. The twenty-one surviving members of the expedition, seven men in each boat, set sail.

They could hardly have sailed into worse conditions. Gales blew; fogs rolled in; ice jammed against the shore and made progress all but impossible. The first day they got eight miles on the way; thereafter they fought for every inch. Much of the time they could not advance at all; occasionally they could win a mile or so by tracking along the beach. On August 27 a hard northwest wind cleared the coast of ice in two hours. The next day at noon the party embarked and proceeded under sail; already they had been four weeks on the way. They passed Batty Bay, just thirty-two miles north of Fury Beach; five days later, on September 2, they were at the northeast corner of North Somerset. There, from a height of land, they looked off and saw Barrow Strait and Lancaster Sound solidly packed with ice; not a pool of water was to be seen. For two and a half weeks they waited hopefully. No one had the heart to suggest going back even though, as the cold weather came and winter set in, it became more and more evident that go back they would have to. On September 25 they gave up hope of the impossible and headed south. They could get no farther than Batty Bay by boat. They cached the boats and manufactured sledges from empty bread crates. On October 7 they were back at Somerset House.

Their fourth winter was terrible even beyond their forebodings. They had the *Fury*'s supplies to draw on, and that meant plenty of flour, sugar, soup, peas, vegetables, pickles, and lime juice. But meat was short and had to be rationed after November 1, and the facilities for making bread were so limited that the men ate a sodden sort of dumpling of flour and water instead. October and November were months of the worst gales yet experienced. The men huddled in their little house, now banked with four feet of snow, and managed somehow to keep warm. Each man had a sleeping place consisting of a strip of canvas and a thrummed mat. At first a single blanket was the sole covering; later, mats were added. No one had enough warm clothes to permit work outside in severe weather. Inside, they could only sit or lie on their bed places and fight despondency and boredom. On November 15 the sun did not appear above the horizon; the winter darkness had begun. Christmas came and went; the men celebrated with a full allowance of meat and the officers shared a fox, but there was nothing to drink but snow water. Scurvy and other illnesses afflicted officers and men alike. On February 22 Chinham Thomas, the carpenter, died. He was buried with due solemnity, though it was not easy to read the service out of doors at 45° below zero, and harder still to dig a grave in the frozen ground. By spring three of the party were so weakened that they could not lift themselves from their bed places; many others could just manage to get about.

With warmer weather, their hopes rose; again they began to dream and talk of escape. In April and May they struggled to carry two months' provisions forward to the boats in Batty Bay. The hauling was done in three stages, the parties having to go back and forth over the same ground eight times, a total distance of 256 miles. It was a heartbreaking task. Through June they waited again for improved traveling conditions and completed the last details of preparation. On July 8 they quit Somerset House and moved forward to the first station, eight miles away. The sick bore the journey well, and on July 12 the whole party was at Batty Bay. There they waited until the 15th of August, when for the first time a lane of water opened, leading north, and they embarked.

What followed was almost beyond belief to the men. In one day's sailing they reached the northeast corner of North Somerset, a trip that had taken five days the year before. The next day, August 17, at three in the morning, they set off across the mouth of Prince Regent Inlet, following one open lane after another through a mass of floating ice. By noon they had rowed within a mile of the northern edge of the ice; minutes later, helped by a southerly wind, they were out of the pack and, after four seemingly endless years in ice-filled waters, once again on an open sea. By three in the afternoon they had crossed the inlet and were running quickly eastward before a fine breeze. They were forced to seek shelter when the breeze heightened to a gale, but they had made a day's run of seventy-two miles and were twelve miles west of Cape York. On the following day, in calm weather, they rowed along the northern shores of Baffin Land as far as the eastern cape of Admiralty Inlet, which they reached at midnight. On the day after, against a strong easterly wind, they made but five miles. For the next five days gales and heavy winds kept them land-bound; it was not until August 26 that they could cross Navy Board Inlet. Ten miles beyond the northwest corner of Bylot Island they found a harbor with a little river flowing into it, and pitched their tents. They had been twelve continuous hours at the oars.

They were now near the entrance of Lancaster Sound, and not too late to fall in with a whaler. Perhaps the rescue they had so long dreamed of was about to come to them. They had not counted heavily on good luck; they had already cut their rations by a third against the possibility of further voyaging or even of a retreat to Somerset House. At the new camp they set themselves at once to make small repairs to the boats; then, with one man on watch, the party slept.

At four in the morning the lookout man, David Wood, thought he saw a sail in the offing. He could not be certain; the white object might be an iceberg or a mirage. He woke Commander Ross, who, with his glass, confirmed Wood's first thought; the white spot on the horizon was a sail. The men were hailed from the tents. Wet powder was set burning to make smoke signals; camp was broken; the boats were loaded. The smoke signals apparently were in vain; they brought no response from the ship. At six o'clock the party was on the water, each boat with its sails set and men at the oars as well. The going, Ross later wrote, "was tedious, owing to alternate calms, and light airs blowing in every direction . . ." By the ship itself no wind stirred; if she stayed becalmed, there was every chance of getting to her. The boats made good progress and the men's hopes were running high; then a sudden breeze filled the ship's sails, and without a sign of recognition she was off to the southeast. The foremost of Ross's boats trailed far behind; the other two turned eastward to try to cut the vessel off. The hours of morning passed; the ship stayed in sight, but the distance between her and the boats could not be shortened.

At ten o'clock another sail was sighted to the north; the ship looked like a whaler lying to for her boats. While Ross watched, the ship hove to; Ross's party had surely been seen and would now be saved. The next moment disappointment came; the ship turned down wind and began to move off. The three boats followed, but again the distance between ship and boats could not be closed. Then the reverse of what had happened to the first ship happened to the second: a dead calm fell. Ross and his men began to gain on her. At eleven o'clock she hove to; a boat was lowered over her side; there was no doubt now what the outcome would be. Soon the boats of rescuers and rescued were alongside; by noon everyone was aboard the whaler. For the men of the *Victory* their adventure in the North was at an end.

Strangely, the ship that picked the party up and carried Ross back to England was the *Isabella* of Hull, the ship that Ross himself had commanded on his first arctic voyage.

3.

Now we go back a year to 1832. All England was disturbed over the fate of Ross. For three years there had been no word of him, and it was being openly suggested that his expedition had met with disaster. George Ross, worried about his brother and his son, petitioned the Government to contribute to a search expedition. The Government answered with a grant of two thousand pounds. Another three thousand was raised by subscription; the Hudson's Bay Company pledged the necessary supplies and canoes; Captain George Back agreed to command the expedition.

The plan of action was daring and imaginative in the extreme. Indian stories had it that not far from the eastern end of Great Slave Lake rose a river known as the Thleweechoh-desseth or Great Fish River. This river flowed eastward and northward into the Polar Sea, somewhere, according to the Indians' descriptions, between the 90th and 100th degrees of west longitude, in the neighborhood of Kikerktak and Prince Regent Inlet. Back planned to descend this unexplored river to the sea and from its outlet to lay a course for Fury Beach, where certainly either Ross himself or some word from him would be found. The journey held no terrors for Back, even though the river, with its supposed source two hundred miles directly south of the Hood River, must flow through country similar to the Barren Lands of Franklin's—and Back's—terrible march of 1821.

Captain Back, with Doctor R. King and three English sailors, two of them carpenters and one a shipwright, left Liverpool on the 17th of February, 1833. Thirty-five days later they landed in New York. From there they went by steamboat to Albany and then to Montreal by coaches or wagons, whichever best suited the roads. At Montreal, Back engaged four privates of the Royal Artillery to accompany him—one of them, William Malley, as his personal servant. At Montreal, too, he discovered that danger did not necessarily lurk only in the North: the hotel at which he was staying burned down. The occupants escaped, some by the second-story windows, and all Back's personal luggage was saved; the worst loss was his barometer, which unfortunately could not be replaced. The next day, April 25, the party embarked in canoes for the Great Lakes and Norway House at the northern end of Lake Winnipeg. Fifty-four days later they reached their destination.

At Norway House, Back met Thomas Simpson, first cousin to George Simpson, governor of the Hudson's Bay Company's territories. Young Thomas Simpson had been a servant of the company in Canada for four years; he was himself beginning to dream of a journey to the arctic coast. He put himself at Back's disposal and helped particularly in engaging eleven suitable men. At the same time he looked at the British naval officer with an appraising eye and wrote: "He seems a very easy and affable man; deficient, I should say, in that commanding manner with the people so necessary in this savage country. From my soul I wish them every success in the generous and humane objects of the expedition; but cannot venture an opinion upon its probable result."

The party now had its full complement—two officers and eighteen men. They left Norway House on June 28 and a week later reached Cumberland House, where 10,000 pounds of supplies and two bateaux for the northern journey were waiting for them. Here the party separated, Back, traveling with eight men in a canoe, to push ahead and search out the source of the Great Fish River; Doctor King, commanding the rest of the party, to follow at the slower pace of the bateaux. King was to pick up an additional thousand pounds of pemmican at Ile à la Crosse and rejoin Back at the eastern end of Great Slave Lake.

As far as Fort Resolution on Great Slave Lake, Back's way was familiar; he had been over it before with Franklin. It took him slightly north of west across the middle of present-day Saskatchewan, past Sturgeon River, Beaver Lake and Pelican Lake, to Ile à la Crosse. There it turned northward to Clear Lake, Buffalo Lake and Methye Lake, then across Portage la Loche—the divide between the waters that flow into Hudson Bay and those that go to the Polar Sea. From the end of this fourteen-mile portage it took him to the Clearwater River, then to the Athabasca, and on down to Fort Chipewyan. He arrived so early one morning that his canoe, despite the crimson flag it was flying, was unnoticed until it was nearly at the fort. Two days later he was headed down the Slave River to Great Slave Lake. Halfway between Athabasca Lake and Great Slave he turned off up the Salt River to look for a spot he remembered from thirteen years before. In time he found it, a low hill with three springs bubbling at its foot. Where the water came out of the ground were sparkling, white hummocks of the purest salt. He filled five large bags. Then he returned to the Slave River and continued to Fort Resolution, which he reached on August 8.

Soon the Indians were telling him stories about the river he had come so far to find—stories from which he could take little comfort. The Indians described the Great Fish River as full of dangerous rapids and narrows and falls, and more winding and twisting than any other river known to the oldest of their tribe. They advised Back to put the river out of his mind as a route to the sea; if he insisted on trying it, none of their people would go with him. However, they said in softer tones, there was another river, the Thelon, which emptied into the sea not far from the mouth of the Great Fish River. The Thelon ran through a country rich in game, and for much of its length was bordered with pines and birches. If a man was determined to travel to the Arctic Sea, the Thelon was the river to take. And again they begged him to stay away from the Thleweechohdesseth.

It was not easy to go against such native advice, but logic came to Back's rescue. If the Thelon had trees along its bank, it could not possibly flow northeastward across the Barren Lands where no trees grew. The Indians must be mistaken; a river that flowed northward and eastward through trees would almost certainly end in Hudson Bay. In this Back was correct. With the Thelon eliminated, there was nothing to do but find the source of the Great Fish River, wherever it might lie, and follow that river, dangerous as the Indians declared it, to the Polar Sea.

Back had already abandoned any hope of getting to Fury Beach that season. Ross, it seemed, would have to wait out another winter before his rescuers came. On August 11, Back, in his canoe, accompanied by his servant William Malley, one Canadian, two half-breeds and two Indians, left Fort Resolution. On August 18 the party reached the eastern extreme of Great Slave Lake, and the next day started up the Hoar Frost River.

The object of their search lay somewhere to the northeast. Indians had told Back that the river rose in a country of sand hills; their guide had been there as a child, but his memory of the place was no longer clear. For a land so vast and featureless, such vague recollections were little enough to go on, but suffice they had to. The first step of their journey, the ascent of the Hoar Frost, was more than they had bargained for. They found themselves among high crags and towering cliffs, where the river fell in one waterfall after another; around each, and always upwards, they had to lug their canoe, their baggage and themselves. Their faces streamed with blood from mosquito and sand-fly bites. At the end of the second day they reached the stream's source and stopped to repair their canoe. From the Hoar Frost north the country was not quite so steep. On streams broken with rapids but still passable to canoe, the party went on from one lake to another; the weather grew steadily colder; the men saw caribou and white wolves and "white partridge."

On August 24 they entered Lake Clinton-Colden, magnificent in size, its water deep indigo and very clear. Ice along its western shore warned Back of how long winter hung on in the Barren Lands and of how faint a chance he had of starting his next year's open water journey during the early part of the summer. The guide now felt sure they were on the right track and would soon see sand hills; he was wrong.

The next day they came to the end of the lake, where there was a strait, marked by a lone conical mound of sand some 200 feet high. From the top of the mound they saw another vast lake, Aylmer Lake of today, stretching to the west and north. Was there no end to how far they would have to go? The guide grew less and less certain of the way; for two days more they worked their canoe past rocky islands in the lake and across the mouths of wide bays, none of them familiar to the guide. On the third day, a cluster of sand hills came into view to the north, and once again the guide was confident of his bearings. The party landed and made camp, and after a hurried meal Back dispatched his guide and three men, with three days' provisions, to look for the river's source.

Back himself stayed behind to keep an eye on the canoe and the equipment. During the first day, after scanning the sand hills in vain for any signs of his men, he amused himself by sketching the country immediately to the north of the camp. About a quarter of a mile away was a little lake with a small island in it; there were surrounding sand hills; and beyond the hills north of the lake were bigger hills, the tops of which were rounded cones of sand. Somewhere, in among those hills, probably lay the source of the Great Fish River. The second day Back grew uneasy about his men and went to look for them. From the top of a low hill a short distance from the camp, he looked across the lake he had sketched the day before; in the stream that ran out of it, he saw the froth of rapids—rapids that descended to the northeast. The stream he was looking at did not run back to Great Slave Lake; it ran northward and eastward toward the Polar Sea. He was at the divide; the little lake he had sketched was itself the source of the Thleweechohdesseth. He waded through the swampy sedge of the lake's shore, across two north-flowing rivulets, and came to the stream that flowed east and north. He threw himself down on its banks and drank deep from the water.

Within the next hour Back found a vantage point from which he could see his river enter the immense open spaces of the Barren Lands. Still not catching sight of his men, he lit the tundra moss. From behind the sand hills a column of dense smoke answered his. When the men returned they came with the head of a musk ox, a good fat deer, and the news that they too had come upon the river and had found it wide enough for boats. The little lake, then, was indisputably the source of the Great Fish River. To give honor where honor was due, Back changed the lake's name from the homely one of Sand-Hill to the more elegant Sussex, after his Royal Highness the vice-patron of the expedition.

Back wanted to satisfy himself about the river's size. He wanted to be certain that he could get down it the next spring with two boats. The party cached their excess baggage, portaged their canoe to the stream from which Back had drunk, and for two days followed the Great Fish River as far as Musk-Ox Lake. They found the stream amply fed by many tributaries; there was no doubt that eventually it swelled into a river of great size. And if it passed through a range of mountains they saw in the distance, it certainly had all the dangerous rapids and cascades of which the Indians had warned. They could only guess what its actual course was through the vast land that stretched before them and continued beyond the mountains.

The end of summer had come, and flocks of geese, southward bound, warned of the lateness of the season. It was time to head for winter quarters. The party returned to Aylmer

Lake and started down the chain of lakes and rivers and portages to Great Slave Lake. At the narrows between Aylmer and Clinton-Colden Lake they met two Indians, both of whom Back had known in 1821. They were tribesmen of Akaitcho —the same Akaitcho who had failed to supply Fort Enterprise for Franklin. Overjoyed at seeing familiar faces, Back put reproaches of Akaitcho aside and sent the two Indians on their way with greetings and presents for their chief. His party continued to the south end of Clinton-Colden Lake and from there down the length of Artillery Lake. The river flowing out from Artillery was ugly and fast: at a rapids a short distance down it the steersman refused to go on. Back had no choice but to order the canoe abandoned, and the party finished the journey on foot. On September 7 they reached the easternmost tip of Great Slave Lake and found that Mr. McLeod, of the Hudson's Bay post at Fort Resolution, had already put up the frame of their winter house—Fort Reliance. On September 16 Doctor King arrived with the two bateaux; the whole party was together again.

The winter at Fort Reliance was one of trouble and anxiety. Throughout the entire region the hunting was bad, the fishing worse. From near and far the Indians fell back on the fort for support. First came the old and decrepit; then, as the situation worsened, all ages and sizes drifted in. The feeblest and the sickest crowded into the fort itself, the others camped round about. Back hardly knew what to do; his visitors were like a swarm of locusts. To feed them, he set up one fishery after another, but nowhere did the gill nets produce more than a handful of fish. In November Akaitcho appeared, wearing a silver medal given him by Franklin. He did everything he could to relieve the situation. He led the able-bodied Indians to the hunt, and he exerted his prestige to stop the begging, but the whole situation improved little. Back had to dig into his precious pemmican. He doled it out as sparingly as he could and kept an eagle eye on the supply. The more he gave to the Indians, the less there would be for his own journey to the Polar Sea.

The weeks wore on. In midwinter the temperature fell to 70° below zero and lower. It was so cold in the fort that when Back washed his face within three feet of the fire, ice formed in his hair. The skin on the men's hands dried and cracked into deep gashes. Back got what diversion he could from studying magnetism and watching the aurora and from conducting experiments on the effects of extreme cold. In February he started his carpenters on the work of building two boats. The necessary lumber was cut from a stand of pine twelve miles from the fort, then sledged to the foot of Artillery Lake, where actual construction began. Meanwhile the pemmican supply for the northern voyage diminished from sixty bags to twenty-five; Back began to wonder if he would have any at all left by spring.

In the middle of March an Indian came into camp with two sledges of dried meat; thereafter, as the weather grew milder, the demands on Back lessened somewhat. On April 25 there was an unexpected and loud knock on the door of his quarters. The door opened immediately after the knock, and a messenger thrust a packet at Back and at the same time blurted out: "He is returned, sir!" For Back it was a moment of relief. Months before, Back had been told that an old Eskimo interpreter who had been with him and Franklin in 1821 had heard that he was again in the North and had set out to walk from Churchill to join him. Only a month before,

a messenger had brought word that poor Augustus was lost
and probably dead. Now here was the good news that he
was still alive. "What!" said Back. "Augustus?—thank God!"
The messenger hesitated; he did not want to disappoint Back,
yet he must deliver the real news. He said. "Captain Ross,
sir—Captain Ross is returned!"

The packet he had thrust at Back contained newspaper
clippings about Ross's remarkable escape; also an official letter
which directed Back to survey, if possible, the coast between
Ross's cairn at Victory Point and Point Turnagain. Nothing
could have pleased Back more. He was equally delighted over
Ross's safe return and his own good luck in being able to
continue northward. He had his plans made almost at once.
As soon as the season permitted, he and Doctor King, with
eight men and one boat and what pemmican was left, would
set out to trace the course of the Great Fish River to its outlet
at the sea. If successful, they would end up not far from
Kikerktak itself.

On May 13 "a single goose, the harbinger of summer, flew
past the house." Back knew that in a few weeks he could be
off. In order to get to the Great Fish River early in the season
he planned to start from Fort Reliance before the ice on the
lakes broke up. On June 5 McLeod, who had rejoined Back
after wintering at Fort Resolution, set out for Musk-Ox Lake
with a supporting party to lay down caches and carry baggage. Two days later Back and King, with their men, were
on the way.

The weather was warm and sultry, the temperature in the
sun 107°. The swamps were flooded; the dwarf birches were
budding; the willow catkins were already half an inch long.
At the foot of Artillery Lake the party picked up the bigger

of the two boats Back had ordered built during the winter and added the carpenters to the party; the smaller boat they left in a pool against their return in the autumn. Two men and six dogs dragged the boat, on runners, across the ice of the lake; each of the other men pulled behind him a contraption like a brewer's sledge, loaded with a hundred pounds of miscellaneous gear and provisions. The ice was honeycombed and dangerously thin; the boat was heavy and when the ice was soft, almost impossible to move. The season seemed to advance faster than the men could struggle forward. Ducks and geese and loons flew overhead; caribou were seen in small numbers. The sun was above the horizon twenty out of twenty-four hours, and there was daylight around the clock. To get the coolest air and the firmest ice they traveled by night. The dogs were fitted with little leather shoes to save their feet from ice cuts. Most of the time the men were soaking wet and so tired they often did not care whether they went on or not. If anyone got sick, treatment for his ailment was of the rough-and-ready kind. It worked remarkably well; a case of blindness, resulting from inflamed eyes and swollen lids, was cured speedily with a couple of drops of laudanum and a "smart cathartic."

The party pushed on, up the length of Artillery Lake and then of Clinton-Colden. They found the narrows leading into Aylmer Lake open, except where the current was weak. They got the boat through partly by water and partly over the ice, with no one escaping a ducking. On Aylmer Lake snow and hail and rain plagued them. Moss and willow twigs were the only fuel, and the meager handfuls of these that could be found were too damp to burn; the men went to bed wet and unwarmed. On the morning of June 27, twenty days after

leaving Fort Reliance, they came to Sand-Hill Bay, where
Back had been camped the year before when he made his
discovery of the Great Fish River's source.

Here, to his dismay, the carpenters warned that the boat,
built of soft pine, could not be dragged across the rough
quarter-mile portage without damage to its keel. Warned earlier, at Fort Reliance, Back could have procured material suitable for a keel; now he could only wonder uneasily if eight
men could carry so heavy a load. They tried—and succeeded.
They shouldered the thirty-foot boat, keel up, and with almost superhuman effort carried it to the waters of the Thleweechohdesseth. Back was amazed and encouraged; with
turbulent rapids and long cascades ahead, other carries were
inevitable. The upper part of the river was difficult: it was
narrow and the rapids shallow. Much of the time the boat
had to be floated downstream empty. There were many portages; where the river widened and the current slackened,
long stretches of ice had to be crossed. Endless times the baggage had to be unloaded and reloaded again. On June 30 they
reached Musk-Ox Lake and joined McLeod and his men. The
four-mile portage at the lake's outlet occupied both parties
for a full day. A short distance down the river from the portage the last partings took place. Akaitcho appeared, waiting
for the party on an island in midstream—to say good-by and
to warn Back once more of the dangers that lay ahead. The
carpenters tightened and calked the boat and, with McLeod
and his men, turned back for Fort Resolution. On July 8 Back
and his party began the descent proper.

Their boat, thirty feet long, had a twenty-four-foot keel.
Her upper part was built of overlapping planks; her lower
part was smooth, so made to be easier to repair and less apt

to catch on rocks in the rapids; the bottom was payed over
with tar. She carried extra oars, masts, and an extra tiller; also
three months' provisions, mostly pemmican—twenty-seven
bags of it, each weighing ninety pounds. McLeod had managed
to add a few bags to the little left of Back's original supply.
The other provisions were scanty in the extreme—two boxes
of macaroni, some flour, a case of cocoa, twelve pounds of
tea and a two-gallon keg of rum. "The weight," wrote Back,
"was calculated at 3360 lbs., exclusive of the boat's covering
or awning, masts, yards, sails, spare oars, poles, planking, and
the crew." This was the load that somehow had to be taken
down an unknown river, supposedly filled with rapids and
cascades of the most dangerous kind.

At ten o'clock in the morning the party embarked. Back
had in mind three places where the river might take him: first,
Bathurst Inlet; second, somewhere near where James Clark
Ross had been; and third, Hudson Bay. If the Great Fish River
reached the Polar Sea at the first or second place, he would
have a chance to survey the coast between Point Turnagain
and Victory Point; if it flowed into Hudson Bay, his only
reward for his efforts would be bitter disappointment, for no
discoveries awaited him there.

For the first eighty miles the river held to a northerly course;
it seemed certain it was going to Bathurst Inlet. Shortly beyond Musk-Ox Lake it had left the mountains and began a
long flow through the broad expanse of the Barren Lands.
Here the banks of the river were white sand; beyond the
banks stretched the prairie, green and swampy and dotted
with herds of musk oxen and caribou; far away, at the horizon, rose grayish hills. Day after day, for seven days, they
went through a land that seemed endless in extent. Now the

river widened, sometimes into frozen lakes, where they had to force, or even cut, their way through; at other times it narrowed through icy gullies and gorges, where there were rapids and cascades, the roar of which could be heard a mile away. The nerve and skill of the two steersmen, Sinclair and M'Kay, never failed; somehow they always managed to get the boat through safe.

From the portage at Musk-Ox Lake, bad weather plagued them; it was foggy and rainy and cold. One bitter gale kept them in camp for two days. Often, because of fog, they could hear rapids but not see them and dared not venture forward. At night Back and King shared a tent, but there was no such luxury for the men: they slept in the open under blankets drenched with rain. On the morning of the sixth day, the sun came out for the first time, and Back stopped to take sights. The crew hurried off in pursuit of a herd of seven hundred caribou. Back's observations showed his position to be eighty miles south of Bathurst Inlet. With any luck at all he would soon be at the Polar Sea. The crew, gone scarcely an hour, came back with four bucks. Then, for breakfast, there was raw marrow, cooked meat, and a thick soup made by boiling down the blood. Everybody's spirits rose, and once more they got into the boat and followed the river on its northward course.

In another twenty miles their hopes of a quick journey to the sea were dashed. Mountains of reddish granite appeared ahead, and the river, hemmed in by almost perpendicular hillsides, turned sharply to the right and emptied into a great lake —Beechey Lake—that extended southeastward as far as the eye could see. It was as if fate had deliberately turned them from their goal. Back looked everywhere for an outlet to the west or north but with no success. There was nothing to do but put up the sail and start down the lake. The countryside grew less rugged and the hills less high; thousands of caribou were seen grazing along the shore. On July 15 they reached the foot of the lake, where the river poured out to the eastward over a series of rapids two miles in length, with a total drop of sixty feet.

Did the new direction and the loss of altitude mean that the river went to Hudson Bay? There was no choice but to follow it and find out. For the next seven days Back and his men voyaged onward, at first nearly due east, then to the northeast. They came to pools filled with fish—just what kind they did not know. The river widened, and great tributaries poured in from both sides; the color of the water changed from clear blue to olive green. For two days they glided through a flat country, where the river banks were low; on one of the days they saw an estimated twenty thousand caribou. The farther they went, the clearer the sky grew and the warmer the days. The temperature rose to 84° in the sun. It seemed certain that they were turning their backs on the north. When they came upon traces of Eskimos—tent rings and stones laid up for markers—Back's gloom deepened. He decided that they were the traces of Eskimos from Chesterfield Inlet, now scarcely 150 miles away.

His mood became more cheerful when, a little farther on, the river widened to over a mile and a half, with a surface broken by innumerable sandbanks and islands and shoals. The conditions reminded Back of the western mouth of the Mackenzie and made him hopeful that their course would soon turn north. They came to a place where willows grew in great thickness along the bank and gave cover to thousands of Canada geese that had recently cast their quill feathers and were consequently unable to fly. Everywhere musk oxen and caribou were plentiful.

Again the river narrowed and entered a gloomy gorge between towering cliffs of red gneiss. All likeness to the Mackenzie vanished, and Back's party found themselves in "a deep and settled gloom in the abyss—the effect of which was heightened by the hollow roar of the rapid, still in deep shade, and by the screaming of three large hawks, which frightened from their aërie were hovering high above the middle of the pass, and gazing fixedly upon the first intruders on their solitude . . ." Back named the rapids Hawk Rapids and found comfort in the thought that the Indians had described just such rapids in a gorge where hawks always made their nests. Perhaps the river would do as the Indians said and empty into the Polar Sea. Then the stream broke out of the gorge and took a more northerly course. Widening, it poured into a great ice-filled lake with many bays. This great body of water Back named Pelly Lake. It was one of the lakes on the Great Fish River that the Indians had described to him; not far beyond it was the "stinking lake," their name for the sea.

Back saw no signs of the sea. Instead, he and his men came to two more vast lakes—Garry and MacDougall. Like Pelly, they were shallow, and in places thickset with hundreds of sandy islands. The river current was hard to find; often there was no current at all. Progress was slow, a matter of chopping or poling or ramming, or even of getting out into waist-deep water and pushing the boat through floating cakes of ice. They came upon more and more signs of Eskimos; to be on the safe side against a possible surprise attack, a watch was set at night. In the narrows between Pelly Lake and Garry Lake they found grayling playing and rising to flies. On July 22 they reached the outlet of MacDougall Lake, only to find that they were no farther north than when they had first started across the lakes four days before.

Here, where the river poured from MacDougall Lake, they came upon not one great waterfall, as the roar had led them to believe, but upon "a succession of falls and cascades, and whatever else is horrible in such 'confusion worse confounded.' It expanded to about the breadth of four hundred yards, having near the centre an insulated rock about three hundred feet high, having the same barren and naked appearance as those on each side. From the projection of the main western shore, which concealed the opening, issued another serpentine rapid and fall; while to the right there was a strife of surge and rock, the roar of which was heard far and wide. The space occupying the centre from the first descent to the island was full of sunken rocks of unequal heights, over which the rapid foamed, and boiled, and rushed with impetuous and deadly fury. At that part it was raised into an arch; while the sides were yawning and cavernous, swallowing huge masses of ice, and then again tossing the splintered fragments high into the air. A more terrific sight could not well be conceived, and the impression which it produced was apparent on the countenances of the men."

The only possible portage was over slippery and uncertain rocks. Even if the men had the strength to carry the boat, they would never be able to keep their footing. There was nothing to do but run the boat down the falls. It was unloaded, and "every precaution that experience could devise was adopted; double lines to the bow and stern were held on shore by the most careful of the men, and M'Kay and Sin-

clair took their stations at each end of the boat with poles, to
keep her from dashing against the rocks. It was no common
attempt, and excited in me the most lively concern for their
safety. Repeatedly did the strength of the current hurl the
boat within an inch of destruction, and as often did these able
and intrepid men ward off the threatened danger." The boat
reached the bottom safe, with no damage but the loss of the
keel plate. On the return of the men to the baggage at the
top of the rapids—now named Rock Rapids—Back ordered
the two-gallon keg of rum broached and a measure of grog
served to all.

The next day they carried the baggage over the portage
and, in the evening, were on their way again. Back had no
more worries on the score of the direction the river took. For
three hundred miles—seven days of traveling—it twisted and
turned and carried the boat northward. One rapid came after
another in quick succession: Sinclair Falls, Escape Rapids,
Wolf Falls, Strong Rapids. As the party went along, the countryside changed; it became rugged and mountainous, with a
dark and purplish hue. On July 26, three days after leaving
Rock Rapids, they crossed the Arctic Circle. The temperature
dropped into the thirties; a cold wind blew; and, to use Back's
own words, "the swollen river now rolled on in sullen and
deathlike silence, long undisturbed by any thing louder than
an occasional bubbling caused by the unevenness of the bottom."

Beyond the mountains they found not the sea, as Back had
expected, but another lake—Franklin Lake. In descending the
rapids out of this lake they came to a place where "the river
became again pent in by almost meeting rocks of considerable
altitude". Here there was a fall, above which, on the eastern

75

bank of the river, stood an Eskimo encampment of three skin tents. Dogs lay basking in the sunshine, and on the rocks round about were thousands of split fish spread out to dry, the roes apparently being particularly prized. The meeting with the natives was friendly. Back presented them with beads and buttons and other such trifles, and in return the Eskimos gave the white men a few bone ornaments. The native men were well knit and athletic and wore flowing beards and "mustachoes." The women were tattooed about the face and on the middle of the fourth finger; "their jet-black hair was neatly combed, and parted in front into two large curls; while the rest was tied up in a roll on each side: and from their ears were suspended portions of the ermine skin, cut into narrow pieces of about two inches in length."

Without an interpreter it was impossible to carry on a conversation. Back did the best he could with the help of a vocabulary taken from Parry's book, but his best was little better than nothing. He got some information about the lay of the land and the general direction of the coast. The Eskimos lent a hand in carrying the boat around the falls, and once more the party was on its way.

The next day, July 29, they reached the sea at the head of Chantrey Inlet. "This then," wrote Back, "may be considered as the mouth of the Thlew-ee-choh, which, after a violent and tortuous course of five hundred and thirty geographical miles, running through an iron-ribbed country without a single tree on the whole line of its banks, expanding into fine large lakes with clear horizons, most embarrassing to the navigator, and broken into falls, cascades, and rapids, to the number of no less than eighty-three in the whole, pours its waters into the Polar Sea. . . ."

76

Back was not content to rest with his achievement; he must push on to Point Turnagain. Much of the inlet, especially the western side, was tightly jammed with ice, but this in no way discouraged him. The east side was open; he followed it north to Cape Beaufort. From there, on August 1, a lead to the west suddenly opened, and in three and a half hours, with sail and oar, they made the crossing to Montreal Island. Here gales and ice held them up for five days. Wind and ice abating, they made Adelaide Peninsula and on August 8, in a boat battered by ice and weakened by hard travel, they reached Point Ogle.

They could hardly have found a more desolate spot on the face of the earth. It was flat and sandy and covered with stones; at high tide its northern tip was cut off from the mainland. To the west, across ice, lay Maconochie Island and Point Richardson. It was in this direction that Back wanted to go. For seven cold, dank days the party, miserably encamped, waited for the ice to open. The second day there was a thunderstorm, followed by fog and icy gales. The men, drenched to the skin, searched everywhere for ferns or moss to burn. For the first three nights they had no fire at all; then they found a piece of driftwood, nine feet long and nine inches in diameter. They called it jokingly a piece of the North Pole; they were glad enough to have its warmth and fire for cooking a hot meal.

On August 11 the weather cleared a little, and for the first time in five days the sun came out for a few minutes. Back, looking north, saw in the distance what he took to be two islands, close together. The western point of these he named Point James Ross, after the man whom he had been sent out from England to save. Four days later, in another sunny spell, he again saw the same two islands, and this time he named the eastern point Point Booth. After that he had little further interest in his discovery; his heart was set on getting west to Point Turnagain. Actually, he had seen not two islands, but separate headlands on the shore of Kikerktak, which now for the first time had been sighted from the south. Back by his efforts had shown beyond doubt that from the land he had glimpsed to the north there lay, up a long river and through a country abounding in game, a route to Great Slave Lake and to an outpost of civilization. To white men caught on Kikerktak or anywhere near by, this route might well prove a possible way of escape.

At the end of a week, with no letup in the foul weather and no signs of a breakup in the ice, all hope of getting westward had to be abandoned. It was August 15, the last date Back dared to linger in the North. On August 16 the party headed for Montreal Island and the mouth of the Great Fish River, to go back by the way they had come. It was disappointing to abandon the quest just as they were entering the North-west Passage region but there was nothing else to do. Five days later they had reached the river; by the middle of September they were at its source; on September 27 they were at Fort Reliance. There they spent the winter, and in March Back set out for England and for home.

As exploration, Back's achievements of 1833-34 were many and great. In tracing the Great Fish River to its mouth he had shown that a third great Barren Lands river, in addition to the Mackenzie and the Coppermine, emptied into the Polar Sea. Although he had not recognized Kikerktak for what it was, he had opened the way to it from the south, and he had come close to linking his own discoveries with those of James Clark Ross.

His daring voyage from the source of the Great Fish River to Point Ogle included one unfortunate incident of which Back knew nothing until his return to England. While at Point Ogle he had sent three men to Mount Barrow to make observations. On the way, when they stopped at a small lake to hunt wild fowl, they were surprised by a party of Eskimos, who fired arrows at them. The men retaliated with gunfire; three natives fell dead and others were wounded. Both sides immediately retreated and did not meet again. It can never be known how much the shooting of that day affected the lives of explorers who came later to search for the Northwest Passage. Back himself did not hear of the fray until his party was back in England, when his men apparently thought it wise—or safe—to tell him of it. It was too late then for Back to make amends to the Eskimos of Point Ogle, or to assure them that not all white men with guns were to be distrusted and avoided.

4.

Back reached England early in September, 1835. Eight months later, in June, 1836, he sailed again for the Arctic, this time in command of the bomb ketch *Terror*, with a complement of fifty-five officers and men. Under Admiralty orders, he was to take the ship to Wager Bay (or Wager River as it was then called), on the west side of Hudson Bay, and from there transport whale boats to the bottom of Prince Regent Inlet. One party was then to survey the eastern side of that inlet up to Fury and Hecla Strait: another was to voyage westward and try to get at least to the estuary of the Great Fish River. This voyage to the westward was a shot in the dark; in the year 1836 no one knew whether Boothia was an island or a peninsula of the mainland. Hope ran high that a navigable passage separated it from the continent. If such a passage existed, then the western boat voyage could not be long, and Back's instructions called for the completion of his work in one season.

Back, it so turned out, never got even to Wager Bay. The summer of 1836 was unusual both for ice and for cold. In August the *Terror* was caught by floes in Frozen Strait, near the entrance to the northern end of Roes Welcome and Repulse Bay. She was held in the strait all winter, rammed and squeezed by ice and all but destroyed. In the spring she drifted slowly with the ice back to Hudson Strait, where, on July 11, 1837, she was released. By then she was so damaged and unseaworthy that it was all she could do to reach the Irish coast, where, after a profitless voyage of fifteen months, she was beached to keep her from sinking. With the beaching of his ship, Back's explorations in the north came to an end.

At the same time that Back sailed from England in the *Terror,* the Hudson's Bay Company was laying plans for an expedition of its own to the Polar Sea. If Back succeeded in reaching the estuary of the Great Fish River, there would then be left only two unexplored stretches of the northern coast—the three hundred and ninety miles between Point Ogle and Point Turnagain, and the one hundred and fifty miles between Return Reef and Point Barrow. These stretches the Hudson's Bay Company hoped to explore. Their expedition was to leave Fort Chipewyan in two small sea boats as soon as the ice broke up in the spring of 1837, descend the Mackenzie, and from that river's mouth follow the coast westward to Point Barrow. The party would then come back and take up winter quarters at the northeast corner of Great Bear Lake. In the spring of 1838 it would go down the Coppermine and trace the shore eastward to Chantrey Inlet, where Back's River pours into the Polar Sea. Such a course—though it was not known at the time—would take the party along the southern shore of Kikerktak, perhaps lead to the realization that Ross's King William Land was an island. If all went well with this small expedition, to it—and to the Hudson's Bay Company—would go the honor and glory of solving the problem of a Northwest Passage.

In command was Chief Factor Peter Warren Dease, a man of nearly fifty who had been with Franklin in 1825-26. But the driving force in the expedition was young Thomas Simpson, twenty-nine, second in command. All he cared about in the world was to complete the Northwest Passage; the expedition was to be his chance. No matter what the struggle, no matter what the odds, he was determined that he, no other, should fill in the last gaps in the passage. Nothing should stop him, not even lugging along an old man like Dease. This was the same Thomas Simpson who, three years before, had met Back at Norway House and coolly sized him up. Now Simpson himself was to try exploration, to put his own abilities to the test. He and Back would be on the arctic coast at the same time. It should be easy to see which of the two men was the better explorer—a point on which Simpson had few, if any, doubts.

At the end of July, 1836, Dease left Norway House for Fort Chipewyan; Simpson went to Red River settlement to brush up on mathematics and practical astronomy. On December 1 he set out to join Dease—a winter journey of 1,277 miles that he completed on foot in forty-six traveling days. He arrived at Fort Chipewyan on February 1, 1837; and for the next four months he and Dease made ready for their voyage. While at the fort Simpson received by the winter express a copy of Back's journal of his Fish River journey. Of it he remarked in his own journal: "It contains, indeed, little thought, with no small portion of French sentimentality and self-admiration; but, altogether, I think he has made the most of his subject, which was not a fertile one."

On the first of June the party was ready to be off. Their boats, the *Castor* and the *Pollux*, were clinker-built, of twenty-four-foot keel and six-foot beam, and furnished with a wash-board; each carried two lugsails. They were payed with a mixture of clear pine resin, which gave them an elegant and light appearance, and were gaily decorated with paints made from the colored earths of the country. Aboard each was a collapsible canoe, consisting of a portable wooden frame and an oiled canvas cover. A third boat, a luggage boat, the *Goliah*, left Chipewyan with the *Castor* and *Pollux*. She and her crew were to proceed only to the northeast corner of Great Bear Lake, where the winter quarters, Fort Confidence, were to be built. The *Castor* and the *Pollux*, each manned by six men, with Dease in charge of one boat and Simpson of the other, counted among their crews three men who had been with Back on his voyage down the Great Fish River—James M'Kay and George Sinclair, steersmen, and Peter Taylor, middle-man.

The Polar Sea, by water, lay 1,500 miles away. It took the party ten days to get to Fort Resolution, where the ice in Great Slave Lake held them up for eleven days. Dease took the delay as opportunity to vaccinate all the young people, Indian and half-breed, at the place. By June 24 the party had reached the head of the Mackenzie, where they camped for the last time. The rest of the way down the river the nights were spent afloat, with the boats lashed together and drifting down the wide stream. Progress was at a good pace; in one forty-eight-hour stretch they made two hundred and fifty miles. Simpson would not tolerate the wasting of a minute. They should reach the sea as soon as possible, to have time and to spare for the long coastal voyage to Point Barrow.

Before parting with the luggage boat at the confluence of the Great Bear River and the Mackenzie, the *Castor* and the

Pollux took on their full supplies—thirty bags of pemmican, weighing ninety pounds each, and 1,120 pounds of Red River flour. Pemmican alone, as a daily ration, soon became distasteful and cloying; mixed with flour and water it made a not unpalatable soup, or "bergoo," as the mixture was called. The sea boats also carried trading goods for barter with the natives —axes, knives, files, needles, buttons, rings, bright-colored beads and other such trinkets. The party had still a week of travel on the Mackenzie beyond the Great Bear River before they could reach the coast, five hundred miles away. On July 5 they crossed the Arctic Circle; on the next day the temperature in the shade was 77°, and thirty degrees higher in the sun. As Simpson wrote: "The majestic river and its high banks were steeped in a flood of light, and, except the diminutive size of the wood, there was nothing in the landscape to suggest the thought that we had penetrated so far into the regions of the north." Indian huts of green branches lined the river banks; whenever the party stopped, the natives came down to the beach to greet them. The women "whined and simpered after their most attractive fashion," and the children, naked, crowded around the gaily painted boats to see the wonders they contained. On the morning of July 9 the party came upon their first Eskimos—four women in an oomiak, a women's boat, with two dogs. At the sight of the white men the women threw off their clothes, leaped ashore, and fled through the willows to safety. At four o'clock in the afternoon of the same day, from the western branch of the river through the delta, the party came to the Arctic Sea.

Simpson now set out to trace the 374 miles of coast to Return Reef, all of it previously explored by Franklin. The sooner he put this stretch behind him, the sooner his own discoveries could begin. For two weeks the party sailed along the low, icebound coast. The weather was miserably cold. Yet only when gales or fog or ice altogether forbade traveling did they make camp; the rest of the time they were in their boats pushing westward. Along the way they came upon many Eskimo encampments, at one of which some of the natives had "light-coloured eyes and complexions, which, if cleansed from grease, might have passed for fair in most parts of Europe." Everything Simpson saw, he made note of in his journal—the flowers, the wild fowl, the tracks of great caribou herds, the many seals, and the bones of an enormous whale with a skull that measured eight feet in breadth. On July 23 they reached Return Reef; they had covered in two weeks a distance that had taken Franklin forty days, and Simpson could write: "I may here mention that our early arrival at the point where our discoveries were to commence, is, under Providence, mainly attributable to our inflexible perseverance in *doubling* these great icy packs, any of which might have confined us a fortnight to the beach, had we chosen to wait for its dispersion, or even till its extent could have been ascertained."

The inflexible perseverance never wavered; it drove the party relentlessly toward their goal. They paused at Return Reef for supper, then resumed the journey. For the next twenty-five hours they were continuously in the boats. The men were sick with heavy colds and sore throats, and they had had nothing to eat since they left Return Reef, but this was no reason to rest. In the twenty-five hours they made the extraordinary run of seventy-five miles, or half the way to Point Barrow. Simpson was in high spirits; nothing could keep him from success now. Soon he would open the western entrance to the Northwest Passage. The second day they saw herds of caribou, but could spare no time for the chase. On the third day the weather grew dark and stormy and so cold that the boats were encrusted with ice. Progress was slower, Simpson's spirits not so high. The little boats were tossed and squeezed, but each bailing proved them still perfectly tight. With fifty-five miles of shore line between them and Point Barrow, they came to an almost impenetrable body of ice that stretched along the whole coast. For four days they made no more than four miles; it was impossible to go ahead except at a snail's pace. Time was running short. They could not risk a late-season return to the Mackenzie; if they got back to the Great Bear River after freeze-up, they could not reach their winter quarters at Fort Confidence.

Simpson had no idea of giving up; he would explore the remaining fifty-one miles to Point Barrow on foot. The men unanimously volunteered to accompany him, and he chose five. The others stayed with Dease, who, in order to secure the safe retreat of the party, "handsomely"—as Simpson put it—"consented to remain with the boats. . . ." Perhaps Dease was beginning to feel his years; perhaps he was tired of being driven on by a younger man who made so little effort to hide his impatience and sense of his own superiority.

On August 1 the foot party under Simpson set out from Boat Extreme. Their provisions "consisted of pemican and flour; besides which, each man carried his blanket, spare shoes, gun, and ammunition. A single kettle and a couple of axes sufficed for us all. . . ." For water travel they took one of the canvas canoes, assembled. Simpson figured the load carried by each man was between forty and fifty pounds, which, in his inevitable critical comment, was "about a quarter of the weight carried by the voyageurs across the portages of the interior." The day of the start from camp was dark and foggy, with a cutting north wind. The party, like shadow men, moved off along the coast. They forded one salt creek after another; most of the time they were wet to the waist. Deep rivers and wide bays they crossed in the portable canoe, two trips being needed to ferry all to the farther side. They covered twenty miles the first day, making camp at seven in the evening, "half-congealed by the cold wet fog and wind, which incrusted our clothes with hoar-frost and ice, as in the severity of winter."

The next day, ten miles along from their first night's camp, they came to an Eskimo encampment, on a point where the land turned to the eastward of south. Ahead lay an immense inlet. Its depth could only be guessed; the width, before their eyes, was boundless. Simpson was discouraged. With the new trend of the coast, the journey could hardly be accomplished in any reasonable time if they followed the shore on foot. But the water was free of ice. If they could borrow a native oomiak, they could sail across. The women agreed to lend one, and with it four slender oars and two paddles. After getting from one of the women a sketch of the inlet, Simpson loaded his party and the baggage into the skin boat.

That afternoon, in a fog so thick they had to steer by compass, they set out across the bay. A gale blew from the northeast and the waves ran high, but the oomiak was as buoyant as a cork. When night came they pulled the boat up to the shore and slept in its shelter. The next morning the weather cleared for long enough to allow observations, and Simpson determined that he was not far from his goal. Nothing could stop him now. Soon they were in ice again, but the oomiak's shallow draft—six inches at the most—allowed them to work their way through the water between the ice and the shore. Again they encountered a dense fog, one that did not clear until seven in the evening. The coast was now a succession of frozen-mud banks, ten to fifteen feet high. Judged by the distance they had traveled, Point Barrow could not be far away; soon it would be in sight. The evening was calm; ducks flew westward in long files; and young ice had formed on every open space—a warning of the lateness of the season.

The daylight faded and the sun dropped below the horizon, but still Simpson pushed on. At one in the morning of August 4, just as the sun was reappearing, he saw, from the bottom of Elson Bay, the northward stretch of Point Barrow—a long, low spit of gravel and coarse sand. The bay water was covered with a tough coat of new ice; they broke out a passage and forced their way through half a mile of pack ice to the shore. "On reaching it," Simpson later wrote in his journal, "and seeing the ocean spreading far and wide to the southwest, we unfurled our flag, and with three enthusiastic cheers took possession of our discoveries in his Majesty's name." Simpson had proved himself in arctic exploration; to him and no other belonged the honor of opening the way through the Arctic from the west.

Point Barrow itself was a dreary and depressing sight. The first thing that met their eyes was an immense Eskimo cemetery filled with exposed bodies; not far off was an Eskimo village and summer camp. They spent a day with the natives and slept the night at the native camp. Simpson, as he looked to the west and saw a broad lane of open water, sighed with regret that he could not continue westward. "So inviting was the prospect in that direction, that I would not have hesitated a moment to prosecute the voyage to Behring's Strait, and the Russian settlements, in my skin canoe. I could scarcely, in fact, suppress an indefinite feeling of regret that all was already done."

On August 5 Simpson started back; he had 1,150 miles to go to winter quarters. The morning of the next day he was at Boat Extreme, and the whole party was together again. There, high up on the shore, Simpson left the oomiak for its owners to find. Shortly after noon on the same day the expedition headed eastward; eleven days later it was at the mouth of the Mackenzie. For the up-river journey the crews were divided into two parties, each of which towed the boats for an hour, then rested while the others did the pulling. On this schedule they made thirty to forty miles a day. On August 28 they reached Fort Good Hope, where Dease's wife, niece, and granddaughter joined the party. Almost a month later— September 23—they arrived safe at the infant establishment of Fort Confidence, at the northeast corner of Great Bear Lake. The ground was already covered with snow; Dease River was frozen fast; and "a solitary Canada goose, the very last straggler of the rear-guard flew past to the southward."

Almost at once Fort Confidence was besieged by sick and starving Indians. During October and November Simpson spent all his time hunting, in a desperate effort to assure the food supply. Early in December men from the Dogrib Indians brought him disturbing news: they had recently seen the tracks of round snowshoes and the smoke of distant fires. To Simpson, who had no knowledge of Back's failure, the news came as a jolt. Were some of Back's men, overtaken by winter on the coast, wandering across the Barren Lands in search of food and shelter? Had these men perhaps reached

Point Turnagain and already closed the last gap in the North-west Passage? Had Back won the honor so dearly sought by Simpson for himself? Simpson had some unhappy hours before investigation proved the Indians' story highly exaggerated, and grounded only on the snowshoe prints of a Company messenger bound from Fort Norman to Fort Confidence with a long-looked-for packet.

The winter was severe, with three feet of snow on the level and exceptionally low temperatures. The sun did not rise above the horizon from the last day of November until January 12. On March 11 the thermometer showed sixty degrees below zero. No one starved. The fisheries produced whitefish in good quantity, a few trout of various sizes up to fifty pounds, small sucking carp, an occasional pike. After the first of the year each man's daily ration was ten to twelve pounds of venison, or four or five whitefish weighing fifteen to twenty pounds in all. Of Dease, Simpson wrote in his journal of the winter: "Mr. Dease and I live together on the happiest footing; his old wife, a little grandchild, and a strapping wench, a daughter of his brother Charles, joining our mess. Dease is a worthy, indolent, illiterate soul, and moves just as I give the impulse." When tired of writing and chart-drawing and astronomy, Simpson read in the little library he had brought along. In addition to scientific books and books on northern travel it contained "Plutarch, Hume, Robertson, Gibbon, Shakespeare, Smollett, and dear Sir Walter." He waited impatiently for spring to come, that he might be on his way to Point Turnagain and the estuary of the Great Fish River. Late in March he set out to explore the route to the Coppermine, to determine how best to get the boats across from Great Bear Lake to that river. He decided to follow the Dease River to its source, from there a portage six miles to the western end of the Dismal Lakes, and to follow them to the Kendall River and go down that river to the Coppermine—a total distance of one hundred and fifteen miles.

On June 6, 1838, Simpson's party departed from Fort Confidence, with many of the party's members doubtful of the wisdom of Simpson's choice of route. The ascent of the Dease River proved an arduous task. The stream was a succession of rapids; enormous snowdrifts lined the banks and overhung them; willows and other trees grew almost to the water's edge and made tracking on shore all but impossible. More often than not the men pulled half submerged in the icy water. On June 12 they reached the river's source and began the portage to the Dismal Lakes. The lakes were still frozen solid, the hills around them glistening with snow. Transporting men, boats, and baggage across the six miles between the lakes and Dease River cost Simpson and his men five days. On June 18, at four o'clock in the morning, they were on the way again, the boats, loaded with the oars and baggage, riding now on stout iron-shod sledges. Simpson, with his usual efficiency, had brought the sledges up the Dease and over the portage to speed his passage across waters he knew would still be frozen. "We hoisted the sails to a fair wind, and, placing the crews at the drag-ropes, set out at the rate of two knots an hour over the ice, colours flying." The following day they were at the source of the Kendall River; they had made thirty miles. Late in the afternoon of the next day they emerged from the steep, rocky chasm through which the Kendall rushes into the Coppermine. They were over the most dreaded leg of the journey;

the men rejoiced. Again Simpson had proved the soundness of his judgment. Now only the descent of the Coppermine lay between his party and the Polar Sea.

The great river was silent, still covered with ice. But the breakup could not be far away. Spring was in the air; the catkins on the willows were nearly an inch long; a few mosquitoes flitted about; and in the evening the temperature went up to 62°. A warm south wind blew the next day. The Kendall rose two feet; the ice in the Coppermine began to loosen, and a narrow channel appeared between the fixed ice and the river's steep western bank. This was enough for Simpson. At ten in the morning the *Castor* and the *Pollux* were on their way downstream, the first white men's craft to make the descent since 1821, when Franklin took his fragile canoes down the turbulent waters.

The mouth of the Coppermine lay some seventy miles to the north; their passage down was not unlike Back's down the Great Fish River. In every little valley along the banks caribou and musk oxen were grazing, some so near that they could be fired on from the boats. Flowers were in bloom everywhere, and the grass and willows were green, a pleasant sight after the long whiteness of winter. Great blocks of ice rode the current beside the boats, so threatening them at one point as to hold the party up for two days. On the fourth day out, shortly before noon, they came in sight of the terrifying rapids that Franklin named Escape Rapids after his canoes had run the steep, rock-filled descent and miraculously survived. One look at the overhanging cliffs convinced Simpson's boatmen that there was no choice but to do as Franklin had done, and run down with a full cargo. "In an instant"—in Simpson's words—"we were in the vortex; and, before we were aware, my boat was borne towards an isolated rock, which the boiling surge almost concealed. To clear it on the outside was no longer possible; our only chance of safety was to run between it and the lofty eastern cliff. The word was passed, and every breath was hushed. A stream, which dashed down upon us over the brow of the precipice more than a hundred feet in height, mingled with the spray that whirled upwards from the rapid, forming a terrific shower-bath. The pass was about eight feet wide, and the error of a single foot on either side would have been instant destruction. As, guided by Sinclair's consummate skill, the boat shot safely through those jaws of death, an involuntary cheer arose." Just above Bloody Falls a barrier of ice stopped them, and they were forced to tarry for five days. On July 1 they reached the mouth of the river and pitched their tents at the ocean's edge.

It was an ocean filled with ice, with the eastward passage tightly blocked. All Simpson's impatience was of no avail; he had to wait. Not until July 17 was the party off for Point Turnagain, a hundred and eighty miles away in a straight line. Only beyond that point would new discoveries begin. It might be that Back had already made these discoveries. If so, a cairn with a message in it at Point Turnagain would tell the tale. It was only human for Simpson to hope that Back had not been there, that his own efforts would not be in vain. He urged his party on, against every obstacle. Ice, fog and gales stopped them for day after day. To find open water they had to go deep down into Bathurst Inlet. It was the story of the year before, but worse. To add to their miseries, they ran out of tobacco—"swamp-tea, pepper, salt, cotton rags, and even oakum, were used to replenish their empty pipes." By August 9 they had struggled to within three miles of Point Turnagain.

93

Here, in a little cove that they named Boathaven, they were again hemmed in by ice. No sign of Back's party was anywhere to be found. An undiscovered coast lay ahead, but Simpson could not move.

Ten days brought no release. Dease, alarmed by the storms and snow and frost, wanted to turn back. Simpson would have none of it. He labeled his companion a man "so much engrossed with family affairs, that he is disposed to risk nothing; and is, therefore, the last man in the world for a discoverer." Having thus relieved his feelings, he prepared to go ahead on foot, as he had done at Boat Extreme. If the boats got free, some of the party, in one of them, were to follow. If none were able to follow him, in ten days he would be back. Simpson set out on August 20; four days later he was at Cape Alexander, the northeast tip of Kent Peninsula— about one hundred and fifty miles from Kikerktak. There "the sea, as if transformed by enchantment, rolled its free waves at my feet, and beyond the reach of vision to the eastward." At the end of the fifth day he had gone twenty-five miles farther. Before him stretched a great bay, running far to the south and studded with islands. Across this bay, he rightly conjectured, lay the way to the estuary of the Great Fish River. He longed to go on, complete his discoveries, and win the honor that now, more than ever, he coveted for himself. But he could not go on without a boat. Even an oomiak would have served his need, but he met no Eskimos from whom to borrow one. Disappointed, but resolved now to complete the Northwest Passage the next year, he turned back, and four days later was at Boathaven.

With favorable winds and clear seas, the party made the return journey to the mouth of the Coppermine in four days.

Simpson's problem then was to get the two boats up the river to a place of safe hiding. He could not risk leaving them on the coast or near Bloody Falls; Eskimos would find them and break them up; his plans for further exploration next year depended on his having the boats. Three earlier travelers—Hearne, Franklin and Richardson—had declared it impossible to get boats up the river. Three of Simpson's own companions —Dease, M'Kay and Sinclair—agreed. Simpson thought otherwise. He was sure that in a river the size of the Coppermine, a lead could somewhere be found for light boats, and that with strong ropes and hard pulling they could be got up the worst of the rapids. From the fury of the breakers along the foot of the precipices in June, he had "inferred the existence, at no great depth, of a narrow projecting ledge of rock, that, bared by the falling of the waters, would afford footing to the towing party. . . ." The ascent was tried, and successfully, but not without great risks and dangers. The *Castor* and the *Pollux* were towed to a point some six miles below the mouth of the Kendall, where they were concealed in a thickly wooded spot. Again Simpson had proved himself right: as he put it, "ten years' experience well applied may be more valuable than that of a lifetime." Such conceit could hardly have endeared him to his companions, even though he had done what he had said he would. From the Kendall River the party trekked across the Barren Lands to Great Bear Lake; on September 14 they were back safe at Fort Confidence.

Almost immediately Simpson encountered opposition to his plans for the next year. Dease wanted to call it quits; Sinclair and others applied for discharge. For a time it seemed that Simpson would be thwarted in his unshakable ambition to complete the Northwest Passage route; in the end he won

Dease and the others to his way. What gave him strength to persist against so many, he does not say. We suspect it was the news, awaiting him at the fort, that Back had failed or, as Simpson himself punned it, "Back, it appears, got 'back' after doing nothing." To complete the Northwest Passage was now a bigger challenge than ever; Simpson would have to go all the way to Fury and Hecla Strait.

The second winter at Fort Confidence was much like the first. There was the problem of feeding the Indians; there was the confirmation, to Simpson's satisfaction, that the aurora borealis made a sound like rustling silk. In the spring Ooligbuck, one of Franklin's Eskimo interpreters, joined the party. With June the frosts were almost over, and the temperatures at midday were from forty to seventy degrees. The snow disappeared almost overnight, and on June 3, Dease River broke up.

On June 15 Simpson and his men, who now included M'Kay and Sinclair, left Fort Confidence. Four days later they were at the hiding place of the boats, where they were held up for two days by bad weather. The river was already clear of ice, and on June 22, in eleven hours, they ran to Bloody Falls without a single portage. There they stayed a few days, as the sea ice had not yet broken up. By July 3, two weeks earlier than the year before, they were away from the mouth of the Coppermine and headed eastward along the coast. Wind and weather and ice conditions favored them. Seventeen days later they were at Boathaven, and on July 27, almost a month earlier than Simpson the year before, they reached the limit of Simpson's foot journey. Ahead of them, to Point Ogle, lay some three hundred miles of unexplored coast. Once more Simpson entered the realm of discovery.

He was determined to push himself and his men to the limit to get beyond the estuary of the Great Fish River. Perhaps he could even get to the Gulf of Boothia—the name given to the southern part of Prince Regent Inlet.

They sailed across great bays, passed the mouths of wide rivers, and nearly lost themselves in mazes of islands. At first the coast, always on their right, was bold, with rocky hills of five hundred feet and higher; farther on it grew low and stony. A crush of ice prevented traveling from August 1 through August 4. On August 5, they were able to work out of the ice, and at ten thirty that night, in camp on an island in Queen Maud Gulf, they saw the first stars, "the atmosphere being beautifully clear." A spell of fine weather followed, and for three days they made excellent progress eastward. On August 8 they swung northward, following a sharp turn in the coast. The longitude for the turn was right; presumably the coast would now go north to Ross's Victory Point. Simpson was prepared to have to double Cape Felix before he could reach the Great Fish River.

All day long they sailed in and out among islands, at times fearful they had lost the mainland itself. Still the coast trended steadily north. Suddenly, in the evening, they "opened a strait, running in to the southward of east; whilst the rapid rush of the tide from that quarter left no longer any room to doubt the neighbourhood of an open sea, leading to the mouth of Back's Great Fish River." To their right lay the continent, to their left the shores of Kikerktak. Simpson was justified in thinking luck was with him. The strait might even run through to the Gulf of Boothia. If Boothia were not a peninsula, the distance to Fury and Hecla Strait could not be great. In the water they saw the first salmon since leaving

Coronation Gulf, and everywhere seals were in abundance.

On August 11 they sailed through the strait, the first party to approach Kikerktak from the west. The strait was filled with islands, on the larger of which caribou were grazing. On the shore of Kikerktak, as well as on the mainland, were herds of these animals and many of the stone pillars used by Eskimos in the hunt. Later in the afternoon the party came out of the strait into the eastern sea, as Simpson called the great body of water into which the strait opened. The next day a heavy thunderstorm burst upon them, with torrents of rain and violent showers of hail. They ran for cover into Thunder Cove, where Simpson made observations with his dipping needle. In the morning they were off before a strong west wind, in a dense cold fog. They doubled low, sandy Point Ogle and sought shelter in its lee, but visibility was so poor for a time that Sinclair and M'Kay failed to recognize the place they had visited with Back.

Three days later, with flags flying, they landed at Montreal Island, in a little bay where, five years before to the day, Back had camped. Here M'Kay uncovered a cache made by the previous expedition—two large bags of pemmican, several pounds of chocolate, two canisters of gunpowder, a box of percussion caps, and an old japanned tin vasculum with three large fishhooks in it. The pemmican was full of maggots; the chocolate, though wrapped in oilskin, was so rotten that the men could get hardly a kettleful out of it.

The expedition had fulfilled its prime purpose: it had completed exploration of the coast from Point Barrow to the estuary of Great Fish River. But Simpson could not rest content. August 20 was the date set for the party's return; in the four days left before that date he might be able to discover whether or not Boothia was connected with the mainland. If it were not, then another summer's voyage, probably down the Great Fish River and eastward from its mouth, would get an expedition through to Fury and Hecla Strait. Even during his first winter at Fort Confidence Simpson had thought such an expedition might be necessary. Now it began to seem that he had figured correctly. On the other side of Chantrey Inlet he saw through his telescope a line of high land trending off to the northeast—a true beckoning on. The men agreed to advance; at nine o'clock that evening, without even a night's rest on the island, the party struck out for the farthest visible land.

"It was," as Simpson described it, "a lovely night. The fury of the north lay chained in repose. The Harp, the Eagle, the Charioteer, and many other bright constellations gemmed the sky and sparkled on the waters, while the high Polar star seemed to crown the glorious vault above us. The passage occupied six hours' unremitting labour at the oar; and long before morning we were almost drenched with the heavy dew, whilst the rising swell indicated the approach of another gale."

At sunrise they touched the land Simpson had seen on the eastern side of Chantrey Inlet and climbed up a bluff to get the lay of the land. They had hardly re-embarked when a gale blew up out of the northeast, and it was all they could do to make the farthest angle of Cape Britannia, three miles off, where they were windbound for two days. On the beetling rock above their camp they built a huge cairn of heavy stones, fourteen feet high, and in it placed a sealed bottle containing a record of their voyage. Simpson regretted not having any liquor; the occasion called for a round of grog. Sinclair, down sick, would have benefited particularly. He was brought around by medicines Simpson did have, and no one else in the party came down with his illness. A break in the weather made it possible to gather moss and dry seaweed; a fire and hot meals strengthened everyone.

On August 19 they set sail at an early hour. Boothia could not be too far away; Simpson still hoped to get to it, or at least near enough to see whether it was a peninsula or not. This was the last day they could go forward; on the morrow they would have to turn back. With oar and sail they made a run of thirty miles to Cape Selkirk, where they had their first meal of the day at 4:00 P.M. They then went six miles farther by boat and camped. The northeast trend of the coast suggested they were turning up toward Boothia. If they could only gain a few more miles, the geographical truth they sought would be revealed.

The next day the wind returned to its most undesirable quarter, the northeast. The party struggled on for three miles among shoals and breakers and buffeting waves. But the odds against them were too great, and they were forced to seek shelter in a small river. It was obvious that the boats could be got no farther in such weather. It was evident, too, that the time had come to be starting back. But Simpson was not going to give up without squeezing out the last mile. While the crews set to work to build a cairn, he and Dease walked to a limestone ridge three miles inland. "Our view of the low main-shore," wrote Simpson, "was limited to about five miles, when it seemed to turn off more to the right. Far without, lay several lofty islands; and in the northeast, more distant still, appeared some high blue land: this, which we designated as Cape Sir John Ross, is in all probability one of the southeastern promontories of Boothia." For Simpson, the islands were in the Gulf of Boothia, into which—so he thought—ran the waterway he had been following; Boothia itself was not connected with the mainland. Today we know that Simpson was mistaken: the distant high blue land he saw was probably the high land northeast of Shepherd Bay, and what he took for islands in the Gulf of Boothia must have been hilltops on the mainland rising from a sea of mist. Simpson's excitement was great; in another year, unburdened by an old man like Dease, he would return and complete the Northwest Passage route. He had looked down the trail to its end; the reward of the quest must surely be his. Soon he and Dease rejoined the party. The cairn was completed, and to the little river by which it stood they gave the name of Castor and Pollux, after the sturdy boats that had carried them so far.

The evening of that same day they were off for home. The wind that had opposed them now carried them on its wings, and by nightfall they were at Cape Britannia. Two days later they had passed Point Ogle and reached Point Richardson. From there, on August 24, they set out to cross to the northern side of the strait—to the islands seen by Back; or, as Simpson put it, "to what had from the continent looked like islands, but which I had rightly conjectured to be part of the southern shore of Boothia." Was Kikerktak again fated not to be its island self? Ross had pictured it as part of the continent; now Simpson saw it as connected to Boothia by a narrow isthmus and as making, with Boothia, one big island mass, separated from the continent by a waterway. In either case there was no Rae Strait—no way to the south out of the sea which Ooblooria had said was free of ice all summer. Perhaps when Simpson got to Kikerktak he would discover his mistake. There was still time. He reached Point James Ross and found it not on an island but, as he had conjectured, part of an extensive coast. He never bothered to turn east; he believed he was right about being on a part of Boothia. On his chart he drew in a solid coastline eastward from Point James Ross to Point Booth, and from there on a dotted coastline all the way to the Cape Sir John Ross that he and Dease had seen. There was, for Simpson, no Kikerktak. It was a little as if his conjectures, beyond all question, were always right.

From Point James Ross the party sailed westward along the shore of Kikerktak for nearly sixty miles. Simpson, like Ross, saw no natives, no one to tell him about the land to which he had come. He found it neither exciting nor beautiful—just another stretch of the North. It was, as he wrote, "a limestone country, low and uninteresting, but abounding in reindeer, musk-cattle, and old native encampments. To seaward a good deal of ice appeared, and vast numbers of snow-geese passed high overhead in long triangular flights, bound for milder skies." The musk ox and the caribou—or reindeer, as Simpson called them—were there in plenty, but where were the natives? It was the end of August then; the Kikerktarmiut were probably still at Lake Amitsoq. It was about time for them to start south for Malerualik. If Simpson had come by a month later, he would have met them gathering for the hunt at the place where the caribou cross to the mainland.

On August 25, Simpson was at Cape Herschel. This he took to be the southwest corner of the land he had been traveling along. By observation he found himself only fifty-seven miles from Ross's cairn at Victory Point. He conjectured that the coast turned north and ran directly up there, and so dotted it in on his chart. This merely added to the falsity of his picture of Kikerktak, which he now saw not only connected to Boothia but with the whole of Gore Peninsula lopped off.

On Cape Herschel, Simpson's men built a lofty cairn to commemorate their discoveries, then crossed to the mainland coast and headed for the Coppermine.

A long voyage still lay ahead of them, and winter was fast closing in. As they proceeded westward, they were buffeted by heavy snow squalls; and on September 1 they awoke to find the ground white and the pools among the rocks frozen hard enough to hold a man. On September 5, near the western end of Queen Maud Gulf, they left the coast for Melbourne Island, and from there, at sunset on the evening of the next day, they "stood out thence due north for the nearest point of Victoria Land." This land Simpson had first seen the year before and had named it after the new queen. Now, as he crossed to its shores, he marveled at the strange beauty all about him. "I have seldom seen," he wrote, "anything more brilliant than the phosphoric gleaming of the waves when darkness closed in. The boats seemed to cleave a flood of molten silver; and the spray, dashed from their bows before the fresh breeze, fell back in glittering showers into the deep. It was a cold night; and, when we at last made the land, cliffs faced with everlasting ice obliged us to run on for a couple of leagues before we could take the shore with safety." They followed the southern shore of Victoria Land for over a hundred and eighty miles, then crossed Coronation Gulf, and on September 16, in a bitter frost and with the surrounding country covered with snow, entered the mouth of the Coppermine.

The total length of their coastal voyage was 1,631 miles, the longest that had ever been made in boats on the Polar Sea. At

Bloody Falls they left one of the boats, filled with unneeded supplies, for the Eskimos. The other boat they dragged up the river and left for the Indians. Then, on foot, in deep snow, they crossed to the lower rapids of the Dease River, where a boat was waiting to carry them to Fort Confidence. They reached the fort at dusk on September 24.

Temperatures were falling fast; freeze-up seemed close at hand. If the party wanted to get away that season, it would have to move in a hurry. Two days later they abandoned the fort, and in two boats—one of them the *Goliah*—set out across Great Bear Lake. For four days a storm blew; water froze on the sails, the ropes and the boats, turning everything into shapeless masses of ice. When the men lay down to rest, their clothes froze fast to the planks. It took ten days to get to the mouth of the Great Bear River, and ten days more to ascend the Mackenzie to Fort Simpson, where again they were back in "civilization."

Simpson lost no time in getting at his next year's plans. On October 18 he wrote to the directors of the Hudson's Bay Company in London and asked their sanction of an expedition down the Great Fish River and on to Fury and Hecla Strait, Simpson in command. He was determined that no one should get ahead of him now; he would open the eastern mouth of the Northwest Passage himself and share the fame with no one. After the honor he had already brought to the Hudson's Bay's name, the directors could hardly fail to back him up.

He stayed at Fort Simpson until December 2, when he set out for Red River; he arrived there on February 2. By spring, certainly, he would have an answer to his letter; but if by spring no answer had come, he would go to England and

plead his case in person. On June 2 the spring canoes arrived—
but no letter.

On June 6, in company with a good-sized party, he left
Red River for St. Peter's (now Minneapolis) en route to
England by way of the United States. The progress of the
large party was slow; impatient, Simpson formed a small party
of himself and four others and pushed ahead. On the evening
of June 14 Simpson, apparently under the impression that his
own life was in danger, shot two members of his small party.
The other two fled on horseback to the main party; the following morning, with five companions, they came back to the
scene of the shooting. As they approached Simpson's camp
they called him by name, but there was no answer. They saw
a sudden puff of smoke, and a ball whistled overhead. Who
shot—and why—has never been settled. One story has it that
Simpson shot himself; when the men from the main party rode
into his camp, they found him, so the story goes, still warm,
with the butt of his gun between his legs, the muzzle resting
on his chest, and the top of his head blown off. The supporters
of this story think that Simpson's shooting of his companions
and, next day, of himself can be explained by a madness
brought on by too long a stay in the North and by the disappointment of not hearing from London. Another story says
that the mysterious shot was fired by Simpson in self-defense;
followers of this version believe the suicide story was con-
cocted to cover up a cold-blooded murder. Simpson's rela-
tions with half-breeds had not been good; perhaps an old
grudge had at last come to account. The truth will probably
never be known, but the affair, hardly two weeks before
Simpson's thirty-second birthday, was the end of his haunting

dream of completing the Northwest Passage. He died without knowing that on June 3, in London, the directors of the Hudson's Bay Company had accepted his plan for discovering the last link of the Passage.

PART III
An Island of Tragedy and Search

1.

With Simpson's discoveries, the approaches to Ki-kerktak had been opened from three directions—from the east by Ross, from the south by Back, and from the west by Simpson himself. Only the approach from the north lay unexplored.

On September 12, 1846, twelve miles north of Cape Felix, two ships came to a halt in the heavy ice; they could jam and push their way no farther. They were wooden ships, with black hulls, yellow weatherworks, and white masts. The larger ship was of 370 tons burden, the smaller of 340; and both were barque-rigged—square-rigged on the fore and main masts and fore-and-aft rigged on the mizzen mast. They were broad of beam and bluff of bow, built originally as bomb ketches and designed to withstand the firing of mortars from their decks. Both had previously been on a four-year voyage to the Antarctic, and for that voyage, as a guard against damage from ice, their planking had been doubled and their bows and sterns so reinforced as to be all but solid masses of wood. For the arctic voyage, their bows had been further strengthened with sheets of iron that ran back twenty feet on each side. Each ship had a screw propeller and a 20-horse-power railway engine; in calm weather it could make four knots under steam power. A system of pipes filled with hot salt water supplied heat to the cabins. Aboard were 24 officers and 102 men, all hand picked for arctic service. The ships were named the *Erebus* and the *Terror*; and on the day that they came to a stop in the ice off Cape Felix, they were one year and four months out from England on their way through the Northwest Passage. So far their voyage had been successful. They were but a hundred miles from the known waters of Simpson Strait. From there it would be nothing to get to Bering Strait; one more summer would certainly see them through.

The expedition with a complement of 134 officers and men had left Greenhithe on the Thames on the 19th of May, 1845. In command was Sir John Franklin, of the *Erebus*. After twenty years away from the North, he was back in the Arctic to seek the fame of being first to sail through the passage. In 1845 he was fifty-nine years old, too advanced in age for the rigors of arctic exploration. But the Admiralty believed that his experience in the North more than made up for any lack of youthful vigor. Further, it would have broken his heart had he not got the command of an expedition that had almost every prospect of success. The Admiralty had taken Franklin's feelings into account—and the debt it owed him for his earlier explorations. Second in command was Captain Francis Rawdon Moira Crozier, of the *Terror*. He had been with Parry on his three voyages to the Arctic Archipelago, and he had commanded the *Terror* on her antarctic voyage. Fifty-one years old, he, too, was past the best years for work in the North, but he was unsurpassed in arctic and antarctic experience. The young officers, among them Commander James

Fitzjames and Lieutenant Graham Gore and Lieutenant John Irving, were men with outstanding naval careers, men who had shown their valor and their worth in China and the East Indies and the Middle East. Lieutenant Gore had also seen northern service; he had been with Back on his last expedition to Frozen Strait.

From the Thames the two ships went up the east coast of England to Stromness in Orkney, accompanied by the transport *Baretto Junior*, with additional supplies that she would carry as far as Greenland. At Stromness the ships were watered and took on four bullocks to replace four that had died aboard the transport. She had started from Greenhithe with ten, all to be slaughtered and frozen when the ice was reached. On June 3 the expedition left Stromness; they had a stormy crossing of the North Atlantic and, on June 23, drew near Cape Farewell. They had seen no ice yet, but the weather was getting cold. Two days later they had doubled the Cape and sighted the coast of Greenland. They threaded their way north through heavy ice, and on July 4 reached the Whalefish Islands, with only three of the ten bullocks still alive. At the Whalefish Islands they put in for eight days, during which the *Erebus* and the *Terror* took aboard the supplies on the transport and transferred to the *Baretto Junior* five men who had fallen sick. With five invalided home, the original complement was reduced to one hundred and twenty-nine. They left the Whalefish Islands on July 12 and worked their way along the Greenland coast to the upper part of Baffin Bay. The weather was fine, with every promise of a good ice year. The men's spirits ran high; some of the officers even predicted that the ships would complete the passage that season. By the end of the month the *Erebus* and *Terror* were in the latitude of

Lancaster Sound, but heavy ice prevented a crossing, and they moored to an iceberg to await the loosening of the pack. Two whalers were near by, and the officers of the Franklin expedition made visits to both of them. It was the captain of one of these whalers, Captain Martin of the *Enterprise*, who last saw the ships, still anchored to an iceberg, waiting for their chance to cross Baffin Bay and enter Lancaster Sound.

The Admiralty had instructed Franklin to sail down Lancaster Sound and Barrow Strait as far as Cape Walker. This cape, sighted by Parry in 1819, lay on the south side of Barrow Strait at about 98° west longitude. Peel Sound had not yet been discovered, and many geographers thought that Cape Walker marked the western end of the northern shore of North Somerset. At Cape Walker, Franklin was "to steer to the southward and westward toward Bering Strait in as straight a line as is permitted by the Ice." This route, so the Admiralty thought, would keep Franklin safely away from the heavy ice encountered by Parry farther west, ice in which no ship should risk being caught. Once the *Erebus* and the *Terror* got through from Cape Walker to the American coast, they would be in known waters again; the American coast west of longitude 98° had been mapped all the way to Bering Strait, great stretches of it by Franklin himself. Franklin believed that the Admiralty route was the one most likely to open the Northwest Passage; before sailing, he had pointed on a map to the western end of Simpson Strait and remarked that if he could get there, his troubles would be over. If, however, he should be balked, by ice or for any reason, in his efforts to find a route south from Barrow Strait in the neighborhood of Cape Walker, he had Admiralty orders for an alternative route: he was to sail up Wellington Channel, the entrance to which Parry had shown on his chart, and look for a passage to the north. Many persons still believed in an open sea at the top of the world and thought that a polar route would be the easiest as well as the shortest way of reaching the Pacific.

Their first season out the *Erebus* and the *Terror* failed to get through to the southwest from Barrow Strait. They then tried the alternative route and sailed up Wellington Channel to the 77th degree of north latitude. Finding no open sea, they sailed back down the west side of Cornwallis Island and put in to winter quarters at Beechey Island, just off the southwestern tip of North Devon, near the entrance to Wellington Channel. Compared to Parry, they had failed miserably in getting through the Archipelago, but by circumnavigating Cornwallis Island they had made a considerable contribution to geography; their time had not been wasted. They housed over their ships and prepared for a ten months' stay. Ashore they built an observatory, a carpenter's shop, a storehouse and a forge; quickly and with naval efficiency, they settled into the monotonous routine of a northern winter. The New Year came in sadly, marked by the expedition's first death—that of John Torrington, Leading Stoker in the *Terror*. Three days later John Hartnell, Able Seaman in the *Erebus*, died, and in April William Braine, Private of Marines in the same ship. The dead were buried side by side in neat, simple graves, each marked with an oak headboard and footboard. In spring—or rather in early summer—the men made an oval garden on the east side of the ridge running down the island; they planted the borders of the garden with moss, lichen, poppies and anemones.

In August, 1846, they were on their way again. Ice conditions were good, the weather fine; fortune was favoring them.

In Barrow Strait, just before reaching Cape Walker, they saw a wide channel opening to the south—Peel Sound. If the opening continued to the southward, it would take them to where Franklin wanted to strike the North American coast, near the western end of Simpson Strait. They turned into the sound, and for nearly three hundred miles they sailed southward, their spirits rising with every mile. Again they began to tell one another that they would sail the entire Northwest Passage that season. Under perfect sailing conditions they crowded the ships on. They reached the end of Peel Sound and entered the present-day Franklin Strait; on September 12 they were nearing Cape Felix.

They had Ross's chart and knew with certainty where they were. Down the east side of Cape Felix they saw the alluring prospect of an open sea—the sea that Ooblooria had described as free of ice all summer; down the west side of the cape the channel was packed with heavy ice. But Ross's map and Simpson's map showed the sea on the island's east side as a dead end; Franklin had no choice but to head down the western side, directly into the heavy ice that was part, though he did not know it, of the McClure Strait ice he had been warned to avoid. Through McClure Strait, Melville Sound, and the then unexplored McClintock Channel the ice had drifted down until it piled up on the western coast of Kikerktak. It brought the *Erebus* and the *Terror* to a stop.

Another winter frozen in was nothing to worry about. To be sure, with the distance to known waters so short, it was disappointing not to get through in this second season. They were in sight of Cape Felix; it was twenty miles from there to Victory Point; in a straight line from Victory Point, by Simpson's reckoning, it was but fifty-seven miles to Simpson's cairn at Cape Herschel. When they reached the cairn they would have completed the last unknown link in the passage, and they would have clear sailing the rest of the way to Bering Strait. A second winter in the ice would be tedious and long, but the outlook was bright. The winter could be endured.

The ships were plentifully supplied. They had started with provisions for three years; they had been in the field sixteen months. Even if it took another full twenty months to get to the end of their voyage, they had sufficient supplies to assure ample and varied food. They still had aboard thirty-eight tons of flour and ten tons of biscuit—a pound a day of one or the other for each man. There was enough salt pork to be served two days a week, and an equal ration of salt beef; for the remaining three days there was preserved meat, packed in tins of various sizes up to eight pounds. The bulk of the preserved meat was beef and mutton, but there were tins of veal and ox-cheek and certain mixed varieties. There were plenty of preserved potatoes and carrots and parsnips, and concentrated soups, vegetable and gravy, equivalent to 1,500 gallons, a pint each week for each man. There were 560 pounds of raisins, 1,700 pounds of suet, over two and a half tons of chocolate, 1,310 pounds of tea, and about 625 gallons of lemon juice to be used as a protection against scurvy. There were vinegar and pepper and mustard and pickles in quantity—to say nothing of 2,000 gallons of concentrated spirits and 110 gallons of wine for the sick.

The men were dressed warmly in regulation blue naval uniforms, with greatcoats to match, felt boots, mittens and scarves. In severe weather they wore two pairs of socks and two shirts and two pairs of underwear. They still had with them 3,715 pounds of tobacco and 2,000 pounds of soap, a twenty months' allowance, of 100 pounds a month, for all the dishes and all the clothing and all the bodies of 126 men. And there were 1,500 candles to dispel the gloom of the long arctic nights.

This gloom was the dread of all those in command of arctic expeditions. It fostered melancholy among the men, and melancholy, it was thought, sowed the seeds of scurvy. Everything possible was provided to keep the crews occupied and amused. Both the *Erebus* and the *Terror* carried large libraries, the one on the *Terror* of 1,200 volumes. There were books of all kinds, for all tastes. There were devotional books, Bibles and Prayer Books and Testaments, and there were schoolbooks for evening classes in reading and writing and arithmetic. On each ship was a hand organ that played fifty tunes; ten of them psalms or hymns, the others more lively airs. As further insurance against time's hanging heavy on the men's hands, everything needed for staging plays and publishing a newspaper had been brought along.

With the ships definitely beset, the crews began the work of getting ready for the winter. They housed over the decks with canvas. On the pack they piled up emergency supplies and provisions, against the possibility of a disaster to the ships. They chopped a fire hole in the ice and kept it always open, that plenty of water might be had at a moment's notice. They removed the running rigging of the sails and dismantled all but the lower masts. They left one topmast fidded, on which to run up a light or an electrometer chain. Slowly the *Erebus* and the *Terror* were transformed from ships to houses. No longer were they to be sailed in, on a restless sea; they were to be lived in, on a solid firmament of ice.

It was a comfort to Franklin to know that at Victory Point and at the North Magnetic Pole, only thirty-five miles away, were cairns built by his friend James Clark Ross. They were welcome signposts in an unfamiliar world. More comforting still was the fact that Thomas Blanky, Ice Master on the *Terror*, had himself been first mate on Ross's *Victory*. He had helped with the building of the cairn at the Magnetic Pole, and it was he who had accompanied Ross four hours on foot up the coast north of the Magnetic Pole and helped Ross build a second cairn at their farthest point of advance. If Franklin wanted firsthand information about the part of the world to which his ships had come, Blanky was able and at hand to give it.

At first the imprisoned ships drifted slowly southward with the pack, but soon even this progress stopped. During the shortening days the men enjoyed the relaxation of long walks, occasional polar bear hunts, and even ball games on the ice. On November 26 the sun did not appear above the horizon; it would not be seen again for fifty-two days. The winter routine, with its thousand and one little jobs to keep the men busy, went into effect, and the counting of the days until the sun would come back began. Franklin and Crozier and Fitzjames probed the mysteries of the magnetic force. All three of them were fascinated by it, and to study it with the Magnetic Pole so close at hand was an endless excitement.

On January 17 the sun came back to view; the days grew longer and new hopes stirred within the officers and men. This was to be their year of success. It took patience to wait until the ice broke up, but they were practiced in patience by then. Activity on and around the ships increased; preparations for the days ahead, when the ships would be free, were got under way. By May 15 the midnight sun was in the sky. The snow would soon be melting, the birds coming back, and the flowers on Kikerktak beginning to bloom.

On May 24, 1847, a Monday, a party of two officers and six men left the *Erebus*. In charge was Graham Gore, lieutenant, and Charles Des Voeux, mate. The party was southward bound to trace the western coast and bring back word of ice conditions there. The ships would soon be breaking free, and any information about the route ahead would speed their passage south. With luck the party might be able to survey conditions as far as Simpson's cairn.

Two years had now passed since the *Erebus* and the *Terror* had left England, and they were not yet at Bering Strait. Even when they did arrive there, another six to nine months must go by before news of their arrival could reach England. Before then there could be worry at home over the fate of the expedition. Would it not be well to deposit records along the coast to inform and reassure a search party if one came? These records Fitzjames prepared. The Admiralty had supplied the ships with ordinary tide papers, to be sealed in bottles and dropped into the sea. Recovered, the papers, bearing the position at which they were put into the seas, supplied valuable information on the set of ocean currents. The papers were of legal size, with wide margins. On the lower half of each was printed, in six languages, the request that the finder would note the time and place of recovery, then forward the paper to the Admiralty. The upper half had spaces for the ship's name, the date, and the ship's position, and below these a lined space for further remarks or information. In this space Fitzjames wrote an account of progress to date. The account was brief and touched only salient events; it ended with the words "All well." The forms were rolled up and inserted in tin cylinders, which were capped and sealed with solder. Fitzjames then gave the cylinders to Gore for deposit on the coast of King William Land.

Four days later, on May 28, Gore and his party were at Victory Point. They found the ruins of the cairn, but no sign of Ross's record; Eskimos had probably carried it off. Gore tucked in among the stones one of his own cylinders, then went on his way southward. Thirteen miles farther on, on the south side of Back Bay, he built a cairn and in it deposited a second cylinder. He continued down the coast, to find it trending not directly to Cape Herschel, as Simpson had suggested, but strongly westward; everywhere south of the ships the ice was so heavy and tightly jammed that it looked as if it would never move. When the party got back to the ships, they would have nothing but unfavorable prospects to report.

Their news was not to be the worst news of the season. On June 11, two weeks after Gore left the ships, Sir John Franklin died. The expedition now faced with dismay the future that had looked so bright when Fitzjames rounded off his tide paper message with the inclusive "All well." Crozier took over command, and confidence was somewhat restored. A renewal of optimism followed; in spite of what Gore had seen, the ice might break up late in the season and free the ships in time to get at least to known waters before the end of summer.

June, July and August passed; the ice did not loosen. The year was one of the strange ones that come occasionally to Kikerktak—a year when real summer never came. Instead one winter followed on the heels of another. Slowly the ice drifted southward in a solid mass, taking the ships with it at an almost unnoticeable speed. It was to be measured more in yards each day than in miles. Some of the officers and men set up a camp on the west coast of Kikerktak, three miles south of Cape Felix. On a shingle ridge they pitched three tents and constructed three fireplaces; not far from the camp, they built a huge cairn nine feet in diameter at the base and eight feet high. They had with them heavy clothing and bearskins and sleeping bags, guns and plenty of ammunition, even needles and blue beads for barter with any Eskimos they might meet. Ashore, as a change from the routine and confinement of the ships, they hunted and took scientific observations. Through a system of alignment with stone pillars, they were able to watch and measure the drift of the ships. Down a southwest course the *Erebus* and the *Terror* slowly came, until one day they were opposite the camp, and the next day a little beyond it. Still the ice did not break up; it only carried the ships farther into Victoria Strait. By freeze-up they had drifted nineteen miles in a straight line and lay thirteen miles offshore, opposite Cape Maria Louisa. Simpson Strait was less than a hundred miles away, but any chance of reaching it that summer had gone.

Slowly it broke over the party that the problem of the expedition was no longer one of getting through the Northwest Passage, but one of survival itself. At the most hopeful calculation, the ships were now frozen in for a third winter of ten months, and those ten months would put the party beyond the three years for which it had been provisioned. They could cut rations at once, and the food, eked out, might be made to last through the summer of 1848. But what assurance did they have that the ships would get free then? They knew only one thing with certainty: a fourth winter in the ice could not be risked. To chance such a winter was pure suicide. If they were not to chance it, they must abandon the ships and try, as soon as traveling became possible in the spring, to escape on foot and by small boat. The nearest point of civilization to the south was Fort Resolution on Great Slave Lake, 1,250 miles away by Back's Fish River. The nearest point of help to the north was Lancaster Sound, some five or six hundred miles away; there, in summer, they might run upon such a whaler as had saved Ross, or perhaps upon a search ship. During the long-drawn hours of winter ahead they would have to decide which way they would go. It is small wonder that as darkness settled over the ships and men that autumn of 1847, it brought a cheerlessness deeper than the season's usual gloom. Uppermost in many a mind were thoughts of disaster and death.

The third winter proved horrible even beyond their forebodings. Scurvy attacked the party; nine officers and twelve men died. Time and cold had robbed the lemon juice of its effectiveness. There was only one thing to do: get the men as quickly as possible to where fresh meat could be secured. As Crozier had reason to believe, fresh meat, especially if eaten raw or nearly raw, as the Eskimos ate it, would cure the disease that had struck his party. If he took his men north toward Lancaster Sound, he would have less assurance of finding game than if he took them south; in that direction fresh meat should be plentiful. Back, on his descent of the Great Fish River, had seen musk oxen and caribou beyond all count. Simpson had seen them on both the mainland and the southern shore of King William Land. South was the direction to travel until they came to hunting ground. There they could pause until the sick men had been nursed and fed back to

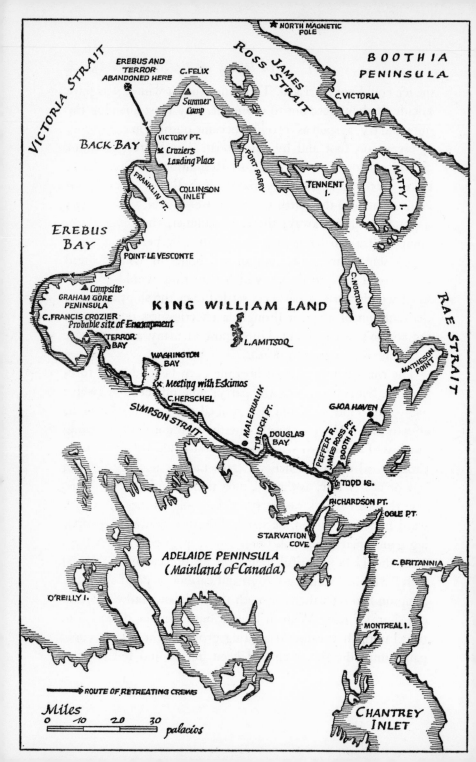

health; once they had regained their strength, the party could make an escape up Back's River to Fort Resolution. They might even meet a search party coming down that river. Back had thought to use it to find Ross. Why should it not be tried again to find Franklin, who had declared the western end of Simpson Strait one of his prime objectives?

The party's departure from the ships had to be put off until the severe weather had moderated. In their depleted condition the men would never have survived winter travel. And before the long journey could be undertaken, boats, gear, and provisions would have to be made ready. Spring would not be far away by the time the men, weaker every day from scurvy, could complete the preparations. Three ship's boats and three sledges formed the core of Crozier's plan for escape. The boats were lightened by substituting, clinker fashion, thin fir planks for the seven upper strakes; so altered, the boats looked like those used by Back on his river trip. Each was 28 feet long, with an extreme beam of 7½ feet and a depth of 2½ feet. Each weighed 800 pounds empty, and over two tons when filled with provisions and equipment. Each rested on a 600-pound oak sledge, 23 feet long and 4 feet wide, heavily shod with iron. The boats were to be dragged to the south of Back's River and then, when the river opened, used for the ascent. It was not the lightest way to travel or the fastest; it was the best that they could devise.

On April 22, 1848, the weather was judged right for traveling, and the one hundred and five surviving officers and men of the Franklin expedition abandoned the ships in which they had set sail from England so highheartedly three years before. Easter fell in the year 1848 on April 23, but they did not wait to have Easter aboard ship. Their condition had become desperate; not a day could be wasted. Their first target was Victory Point, fifteen miles away over rough and hummocky ice. The strongest of the party, harnessed to the drag ropes, pulled the clumsy boats. The feeble and sick rode or straggled behind. The days had now become long; on April 22 the sun rose at 3:23 in the morning and did not set until 8:34 in the evening, and between sunset and sunrise the sky was a twilight sky, never dark. Progress was at a snail's pace. On their first day they covered only a small part of the distance to shore; when they could go no farther they made camp on the frozen sea.

The going was far worse than they had expected; not until the third day were they off what they supposed to be Ross's Victory Point. It was there that they had planned to come ashore. Victory Point was a landmark known to all explorers, a good place to leave a record. Gore, now dead, had already deposited one there. It would be easy to add to it what had happened to the expedition in the ten months since Gore's visit to the point. But when they took observations, they found the point of land that Gore had taken for Victory Point was not in the position given by Ross. According to their calculations Ross's Victory Point, and the cairn he had built on it, lay three or more miles down the coast. They congratulated themselves on figuring this out. Certainly any search party looking for word from the expedition would go to the position that Ross gave for his cairn; finding no record there, it might look no farther.

Crozier sent Lieutenant Irving ashore to get the cylinder Gore had deposited, and the party moved on into a long, shallow bay that stretched toward Cape Jane Franklin. Some three miles south they came to a little point that they calcu-

lated to be very nearly in the latitude and longitude given by
Ross for Victory Point. The new point was small and unim-
pressive, not at all what they had expected Victory Point to
be. They saw no cairn, and when a careful search failed to
disclose even the ruins of one, they set to work and built a
large and conspicuous pillar of stones, five or six hundred feet
back from the shore, where it would be safe against driven ice.
They opened the cylinder with the tide paper in it, and
around the margins Fitzjames wrote a second message. He
signed it, and Crozier added, and signed, another few lines.
They put the paper back and recapped the container without
soldering it. Then they hid the cylinder among the stones
near the top of the new cairn.

The difficult journey from the ships to shore had exposed
the weakness of the party and had made it clear that they could
not continue with such heavy loads. They made camp and
pitched their tents on a long, low ridge between the cairn and
the sea. Then they sorted over their equipment and discarded
everything they did not need—heavy sets of boats' cooking
stoves, pickaxes, shovels, iron hoops, boathooks, staves, and
similar gear. They cast off everything they could possibly
manage without, down to pannikins, clothes brushes, blankets,
extra sledge harnesses, leggings; they even discarded a sextant,
a gun case and a ship's medicine chest. All but a minimum of
essential clothing they laid in a four-foot pile near the cairn.
The decision on what to leave and what to take was not easy;
it was impossible to be certain about what might be most
needed later on. That night, Tuesday, they slept on land. Behind the camp the snow-covered shore rose in a series of
broad terraces to an inland ridge nearly a mile away; except
where the putty-colored limestones showed through at the

terraces' edges the landscape was an unrelieved white. To the north the coast curved out to a long, low point, and a mile and a half to the south was a high, bare ridge that ended at Cape Jane Franklin. Beyond that the land trailed out of sight to the southwest. Their campsite was not the most comfortable, exposed as it was to bitter winds and fog and with the night temperature well below zero. But it could be endured for one night; tomorrow they would be on their way.

They had forty days' provisions—enough to get them near the mouth of Back's Fish River, where the hunting would be good. There they would have to wait until the early part of July for the river to open. In the interval of waiting the men could rest and would regain their strength. The hardest part of the journey would be the first part—the stretch to Cape Herschel. The ice would be rough as far as Simpson Strait; then, in the strait, perhaps smoother. From Cape Herschel to James Ross Point they would be following Simpson's course for sixty miles; from James Ross Point in a straight line to the mouth of Back's River was another eighty-five miles. In all, there lay about three hundred miles between them and the first good hunting they could count on. If they were lucky and found game on the southern coast of King William Land, so much the better. But in his heart each man knew that the whole party could never get as far as the southern coast. Scurvy had a way of taking a sudden turn for the worse, with death following quickly. Many of the men were already near that turning point; they could not last much longer.

The chilling night of April 25 passed; Wednesday morning found the party a little feebler and slower, but camp was broken and all was made ready to go. The men got into their harnesses; the drag ropes tightened; the boats on their lumbering sledges began to move. Ahead, to the southwest, the farthermost visible point of land was Franklin Point, named by Ross in honor of the man who, years later, would die almost within sight of the faraway place named for him. Now the point was the first goal of the retreating crews. If they could get as far as this first goal, they would have some idea what the rest of the journey would be like. Taken by and large, neither officers nor men had ever done any traveling of the present kind before. They were sailors, used to ships and the open sea. Here their natural element lay frozen as if in death, and flimsy tents were all they had for shelter. How often the *Erebus* and the *Terror* must have called them back—back to familiar cabins and decks! Would they have done better to stay with the ships and gamble that during the coming summer the ships would break free? But reason told them that the ships stood for scurvy and certain death; to the south lay a chance, slim though it was, of recovery and life. The start had been made; the journey was under way. Slowly the camp faded from sight; the cairn turned into a tiny dark spot against the snow, visible only from the highest ice hummock; and the hundred and five men went on their way down the western shore of Kikerktak.

2.

From the beginning the march seemed hopeless to many of the men. Gales and snowstorms and impenetrable fogs slowed them and often stopped them; cold and damp sapped their energy. When the sun came out, they were tortured by snow blindness and cracked lips and parched tongues. To progress at all they had to travel close to the shore, where the ice was smoothest, but every twist and turn of the winding coast added to the journey's length. The size of the party was to its disadvantage; at each stop they had to cook 105 meals, boil down snow for 105 drinks of water, and put up cumbersome tents to sleep in. A big tent over twenty-five feet long went with each boat, and in these the men lay down in two rows, feet to feet, their heads toward the sides. Worst burden of all was the heavy boats; all the strength the weakened men could muster barely moved them over the rough ice. Yet the boats had to be taken along; they were as necessary to life as the provisions and supplies they carried. How could the party get up Back's River and across Great Slave Lake without them?

There was always the chance of meeting natives, and this bolstered the men's hopes. Surely, farther south, there would

128

be Eskimos. Simpson had seen their tent rings along the southern shore of King William Land, and Back's party had seen the people themselves near the mouth of the river and again near Point Ogle. Friendly natives could be of the greatest help: they could supply fresh meat and show the way to the best hunting grounds; they might even have word of a search party. The men's picture of their future was not half so black when they painted Eskimos in it; the sooner the Eskimos were met, the better.

The party still had a long way to go to the southern shore after the baggage had been lightened; the distance seemed farther still once the men felt the weight of the boats. The first test of their endurance was the stretch to Franklin Point, and it turned out a cruel test. On the south side of Back Bay two men died and had to be buried. As no graves could be dug in the frozen ground, the bodies were covered with stones. To sailors used to burials at sea, such an interment was almost sacrilegious. To the pain of dying was now added a horror of death. By the time the men reached Franklin Point there was no doubt about the terribleness of their plight. They were weaker and far more scurvy ridden than they had suspected. If the rest of the journey went no better or faster than the first part, forty days would never get them to Back's Fish River.

Day after day fogs and bad weather delayed them and robbed them of precious time. Often they made a new camp only a mile or two down the coast from the camp of the night before. Painfully they dragged and shoved the boats on, past Grover Bay, then around Erebus Bay to its southern side. Here, on an inlet, they made camp again; they were just fifty miles on their way, and it was plain they could not continue as they were. The able could no longer support the burden of the sick;

if any were to get to Back's River or to help, if help were nearer, they would have to leave the sickest behind. It was not an easy decision to make, and everything possible was done to make the decision less harsh for those left behind. Enough well men to care for the sick were left with them, and one of the boats and large tents. There was no idea of forgetting or forsaking those who could not go on. With warmer weather and rest they might get better and be able to follow the main party. If the main party met Eskimos farther along, or if game were found, help would not be long in coming back.

With only two boats now, the traveling party set out around Gore Peninsula. Their progress was slow, little better than before they reduced the party. At last they rounded the peninsula's western end and turned back along the southwest coast. As they had hoped, the ice was smoother and the going better. Had the health of the party improved as it moved to the southward, rounding the farthest west of King William Land would have brought fresh hope. But scurvy had steadily reduced the men's strength. Many who were still able to travel and do a share of the work when they left Erebus Bay were now a serious burden. And every day more men were attacked by the disease. There was nothing to do but find a sheltered place to stop. It was now June; already they had been over a month on the way and had come down the coast but a hundred miles. Simpson's cairn at Cape Herschel was still thirty miles away, and from there to Back's River was one hundred and forty-five miles more.

They turned into Terror Bay and near the bottom of it found just such a sheltered spot as they wanted. On a sandy knoll a little back from the shore they pitched their two big tents, one beside the other. Each tent required three uprights to support it, one at each end and one in the middle of the long ridge pole; the canvas was guyed by ropes fastened to stakes driven into the stony ground. A little distance behind the camp rose two ridges of broken limestone, one to the west and one to the north, each some sixty feet high, sufficient to shut out the cold winds. Along the top of these ridges were pillars of stones set up by the natives for caribou hunting. The sight of the pillars was an encouragement; where Eskimos had hunted before they would probably hunt again. Perhaps with warmer weather they would come.

On the flats between the camp and the ridges were many little ponds. Near one they built a stone wall to serve as a blind from which to shoot ducks and geese. Such fare might not be as welcome as larger game, but at least it was fresh meat. Slowly the snow disappeared from the ground; the last ice went out of the ponds; and everywhere tiny flowers began to bloom—white saxifrage, creamy white dryas, and poppies. The birds they were able to bring down were far from enough to cure their scurvy, or even to arrest it. The sick grew sicker, and even the healthiest showed the early symptoms of the disease. The camping spot that at first had looked so promising began soon to seem a trap. If anyone were to get out of it at all, the party would have to split again.

Forty men went on; the rest stayed behind. Everything was sacrificed to the advancing party. They took as much food as could possibly be spared and the best of the equipment. If they could get through to the continent—to Eskimos and to caribou—all might still be saved, those who advanced and those who stayed. Meanwhile those left behind would have to nurse their strength and live along as best they could. If their supplies failed before help came, the strongest would have to try to get back to the ships for more provisions. Spring was advancing on Kikerktak; the weather was warming; perhaps the men left behind would be able to survive.

The forty men who were to go on were far from strong. They were thin and many were advanced in scurvy, their lips black from hemorrhages, their gums bleeding. They were depressed in spirits and saw the worst in everything. They took with them one boat on its sledge, one big tent, and a smaller sledge loaded with equipment and provisions. The next leg of the journey was the thirty miles to Simpson's cairn. There they might find a message from a search party. That would be the best luck of all, but it seemed almost too much to hope for. The cairn, anyhow, was a goal to struggle toward; when they reached it, they could count one more milestone on the way.

It was a sunny morning late in July before they neared Simpson's cairn. The land was bare; the ice smooth but rotten, with many holes and cracks. The sail of the boat on the sledge was up to catch the breeze, and all the men except one officer were pulling on the drag ropes. From the side of the boat hung a scanty store of fresh provisions, a few ducks and geese that had been shot. Following down the winding coast just north of Cape Herschel, the party turned into a little bay and there, on the shore, saw a scattering of Eskimos, packed up and ready for traveling. The chance the men had so long been waiting for had come.

Their first thought was not to alarm the natives, not to frighten them in any way. It would probably be best if the whole party did not approach them at once. One officer and one man stepped away from the others and turning shoreward, walked toward the natives; the rest of the party moved on slowly, around the bay. The officer and the man advanced until they were near one side of a wide crack in the ice; on the other side, with the water safely between them and the white men, stood two Eskimos, waiting. The officer took every precaution to show that he meant no harm. Still a little way back from the crack, he gave his gun to his companion, who stayed where he was while the officer went forward to the edge of the water. He greeted the Eskimos with their own word of salutation, "Chi-mo," and showed by gesture that his intentions were friendly. When the Eskimos repeated the greeting and did not retreat, the man who had stayed behind put his gun down on the ice and joined the officer. Then, by pantomime, the officer tried to explain that he was hungry and wanted seal meat. The Eskimos appeared to understand and made signs for the white men to come around the end of the crack and join them.

Once with the natives, the officer, again by pantomime, tried to explain the plight of his party—how their ships had been caught in the ice to the northward and why the white men had had to abandon them and try to make their way to the south. If he could only make the Eskimos understand what had happened and how badly off the party was, the Eskimos' help would surely be forthcoming. The officer knew the word for ship, *oomien*, which made explaining a little easier. But the telling of the story taxed his pantomimic abilities to the limit, and when he was through, he was not at all certain how much the natives understood. They were still friendly, and they and the two white men joined forces and walked away from the crack in the ice toward the shore.

Still on the shore were the rest of the Eskimos the white

men had first seen—four families in all, ready to be on the move. The officer lost no time in showing that it was food above all that he wanted. He motioned the natives to open their packs—the men's packs, the women's packs, and the dogs' packs—to show how much seal meat was in them; he opened some of the packs himself. He took out a part of the meat he was shown and directed the natives to load it on a dog's back; then, with his companion and the four Eskimo men, he started back to the main party, now encamped on a little point down the bay. When the men on the point saw the Eskimos coming, they, too, held their arms and open hands above their heads to show that they had no weapons.

While the Eskimo men were with the white men, the Eskimo women set up their tents and made camp, as if they had given up the move they had been started on that morning. The officer who had taken the meat visited the natives in their tents and paid for what he had taken with beads and coins and a knife. In the afternoon some of the men went shooting, others fishing; in the evening, over fires made by burning roots, the white men cooked ducks and salmon for supper, and ate bread, too.

That night, as was their custom, some of the men slept in the big tent and others in the boat. At last they could sleep a little easier. Their troubles were far from over, that they knew, but with Eskimo help everything would be better from now on. The Eskimos could get them seals and tell them where to hunt caribou; they might even carry word of what had happened to Terror Bay and help with the men there. But first of all, the men who were so near Cape Herschel must have rest and a chance to cure their scurvy. With four families of natives close at hand, the place they were in was probably as

good a spot as any for their needs. For a moment the terribleness of what had faced them faded a little; they lay down that
night with new hope, ready for the morrow and new plans.

The morning came, only to bring the one event they had
not dreamed of. When the officer who had first met the
Eskimos stepped out from his tent, he found the four Eskimo
families, all their possessions packed and loaded, on the point
of departure. While the white men still slept, they had broken
camp and prepared to leave. Hardly able to believe his eyes,
the officer spoke to them and pleaded with them to stop. They
gave him no heed. In a last pathetic appeal, he pressed his hand
to his mouth, in the gesture of a man who is starving, and
uttered the Eskimo word for seal. Of this, too, they took no
notice. They moved wordlessly past him and, hurrying on
their way, crossed the shore and disappeared over the top of
an inland ridge.

The white men were now in worse case than if they had met
no Eskimos at all. Hitherto they had had the pleasant dream
of native help; it had been something they could at least pin
their hopes on. Now even that was gone. If they were to meet
natives only to see them run away, what good was there in
meeting them? Probably the Eskimos at the mouth of Back's
River would act just as these first ones had. Suddenly the
journey ahead looked longer and lonelier than ever: they had
hardly the heart to follow it. They left the bay where they
had met the Eskimos and dragged themselves southward. At
Cape Herschel they found Simpson's cairn, but no message;
apparently no one searching for them had come this way yet.
They deposited a record of their own, though it seemed
hardly necessary to do so; any search party from the north
would find the record they had left at Victory Point, and

any search party from the south, down Back's River, they would probably meet and cut off before it reached Cape Herschel. But depositing a record was nevertheless a wise precaution, and once they had taken it, they continued on their journey a little easier in mind. Ahead of them lay sixty miles of coast explored by Simpson, then James Ross Point.

Disappointment over the Eskimos had deadened the party's spirit. They still, of course, had a chance of meeting a search party, but in their despondency the chance looked infinitesimal. What was more, unless they met such a search party soon, they would be past help. They could put some hope in finding caribou on the continent, but first they had to get there. They took comfort, however, in being on known ground, ground for which they had a chart. They could look out for the things that Simpson had seen—the islands, the narrowing of the strait, Eskimo tent rings, caribou or musk oxen. To match what they saw against another white man's description of it gave them a feeling of the familiar—a feeling of not being in quite so strange and faraway a world.

Physical weakness, abetted by discouragement, began to take a steady toll. A short distance east of Cape Herschel the Captain of the Foretop of the *Terror* could go no farther with the others. He stumbled, alone, along the top of a gravel ridge above the beach, where the walking was easiest. After a while he sat down on a rock to rest; perhaps in a moment or two he would feel able to get up and go on. Instead he lost consciousness and fell forward and died. He was not the first person to go in this way, and he was not the last.

They passed the narrowest part of Simpson Strait at Malerualik, where the caribou cross, but they saw none. At Point Tulloch, at the western entrance to Douglas Bay, another man died and was buried. After that, death came to be more and more of a commonplace. It was now summer on Kikerktak, but even the warm weather did not revive the men's failing strength. The ice got more and more rotten, the traveling more exhausting. On an island near the head of Douglas Bay the party camped; here seven more men died. Beyond the Peffer River they had a touch of luck; they found a place where the fishing was good, and the wretched company settled down to rest and savor the fresh food. It had no magic effect; their scurvy was far too advanced for any sudden cure. At this camp they lost two more of their companions, but these they had strength to bury as Christians should be buried, face upward, with hands folded across the breast. Eight miles more on their journey brought them to James Ross Point. At this point on a long, low spit that jutted out into Simpson Strait, the last man to succumb on Kikerktak died—a large, tall man, a victim of the terrible scurvy.

When they left the ships they had dreamed of the day they would be at James Ross Point. It was there that Simpson had first touched King William Land, and it was from there that they would take off on the last, and easiest, stage of their journey to the continent. Now that they were there, how different the circumstances and their feelings were from those of which they had dreamed. Of the one hundred and five men who left the ship, only a handful had reached the place they had thought of as marking the success of their retreat; and the place itself had become just one more place on an endless journey.

The first steppingstones to the continent were the tiny Todd Islands, just off James Ross Point; for them the party headed. On the largest island, Keeuna—the place where one can freeze to death—they stopped and camped. From their camp they clearly saw, due south, a low point of the American shore, hardly twelve miles away. It was Point Ogle, but they thought it Point Richardson; all the points and bays across the strait were shown on the charts they carried, much too far to the east. Through their telescope the coast did not look as it should; the landmarks said they were in one place, the charts said they were in another. To their physical misery and their dejection was now added the confused feeling of being lost, and they were too weak to straighten the way out.

On Keeuna one of the youngest of the party died, and four others. The survivors were too weak to bury the dead; they left the bodies lying close together on a high part of the island. On Keeuna, too, they took from their load every ounce of extra weight they could spare; they even left behind tins of preserved meat.

Still confused by their charts, they started across the strait. Fog made it almost impossible to see, and the drifting floe carried them westward. They did not get into the estuary of Back's River or even into Barrow's Inlet. Instead they entered an inlet on the west side of Point Richardson and there made shore. It was not where they had meant to go, or where they wanted to be. But they did not have the strength to go farther; short of help they no longer even dreamed of, this would have to be their last stopping place.

They pulled their boat up on the low sandy shore and pitched camp. They had shot, and plenty of powder in kegs, and still hoped to live off the land. They struggled to survive as best they could; they shot ducks and geese, but never enough. Slowly the weather grew colder; winter came, and death took its final toll. To the end the men kept with them in their boat a locked tin box, about two feet long and a foot square. In this were the valuable records of the expedition— the results of their scientific observations and the logbooks of the *Erebus* and the *Terror*.

In their last extremity of loneliness, the men who died at the camp west of Point Richardson were nevertheless not alone. Nearby were natives. They were close enough to hear the guns as the white men fired at wild fowl, but they stayed away. Not until the shooting had ceased did they visit the place where it had come from. They saw the last man who died, but they did not make themselves known to him. "He was large and strong, and sat on the sandy beach, his head resting on his hands."

The men who died near Point Richardson were not the last survivors of the Franklin expedition. Before the ice broke up, a party from Terror Bay, with the large boat that had been left at the Terror Bay camp, started back to the ships for needed supplies. They broke their journey at Erebus Bay, where they abandoned their boat and re-formed their relief expedition as a small sledging party in charge of one officer. At Crozier's landing place, the site of the first camp ashore after the expedition abandoned the ships, the officer in charge died. The members of the party wrapped his body in canvas sewed in neat seaman's fashion, and buried him a little eastward of the cairn in which Crozier had left his record. Then those who were left made their way across the ice to the ships.

Here fate played the cruelest trick of all, and there occurred the event that Crozier, when his party was still intact and on the ships, had not dared wait for. The ice broke up, and slowly the two ships drifted southward through Victoria Strait. One, badly damaged, sank in those waters; the other, with the men aboard, drifted on. Toward the end of summer it passed the entrance to Simpson Strait; late in the season, off the west coast of Adelaide Peninsula, near O'Reilly Island, it was frozen in once more. The men aboard had little choice of what to do. For a fourth winter they settled in on their ship. They had plenty of food, plenty of coal for warmth, and, on the great empty vessel, their choice of cabins.

Spring came and once more travel was possible, but by then one man was too ill to move. His companions stayed on the ship with him until he died; then they struck out for civilization. How they hoped to reach it, no one has ever known. They may have planned to go east and try to pick up the trail of the main body of the expedition, or perhaps straight south to the nearest point on Back's Fish River and from there to Great Slave Lake. Whatever their plan, their chance of escape was negligible. Far more likely, they would never get through, but would disappear forever in the vastness of the Barren Lands.

3.

In 1845, when the *Erebus* and the *Terror* sailed from England, twenty years had gone by since Franklin's last journey to the Polar Sea. Less than a week after he had left England on his 1826 expedition his wife died. She had been unwell for some time, but her health had seemed to be improving, and she had urged him to go; for her part she wanted nothing to interfere with his northern plans. The news of her death caught up with him two months after his departure, at a lonely outpost on Lake Huron. He was in the act of finishing a letter to her when the word came. He broke off the letter abruptly and scrawled across the page these words: "Seven o'clock P.M. The distressing news of my dearest wife's death has just reached me." There was nothing Franklin could do but carry on with the expedition, and the next day he and his party left in two canoes for Fort Cumberland, over 1,500 miles away.

In 1845 the *Erebus* had carried Franklin away from his second wife, Jane Griffin, a friend of his first. She was charming and shy and tenderhearted, and she too, when the time came, wanted nothing to stand in the way of his arctic adventures; she knew how much they meant to him and what deep satisfaction they brought. From the day of her marriage in 1828, at the age of thirty-seven, all she thought of, all she truly had at heart, was her husband's happiness and success. For six years, while Franklin served on the *Rainbow* in the Mediterranean, she joined him wherever she could, rejoicing when they could be together, but putting up stoically with long separations when they could not. In 1836 Franklin was appointed Lieutenant-Governor of Van Diemen's Land (present-day Tasmania), and he and Jane lived there, in Hobart, for seven years. They were not peaceful and quiet years, as Sir John and Lady Franklin had hoped, but years turbulent with political strife and storm. Franklin was far from his best under such circumstances; he was no match for political subterfuge and guile. In his own honest and forthright way he did his duty and did it well, but jealousies and cravings for power on the part of his colonial officers brought about his recall in 1843.

He returned to England to find that the Admiralty was considering a new expedition in search of the Northwest Passage. Such an adventure was exactly what he longed for. He wanted the command, and Jane agreed that he ought to have it. It would be like a tonic to him; not only would it get his mind off his Van Diemen's Land troubles, but it would give him a chance to re-establish his reputation with action in a field where his name had always shone. The adventure would be a dangerous one, the more perhaps for a man of his years, and for Jane it would mean a long and trying separation. But what did that matter, so long as her husband could have his dream come true? She was not one to shrink from pleading her husband's cause, not when she thought she could be of help. She wrote to James Clark Ross that of course he himself was the perfect person for the command; but if by any chance he did not want it, might it not be offered to John? "I dread exceedingly," she went on, "the effect on his mind of being without honorable & immediate employment & it is this which enables me to support the idea of parting with him on a service of difficulty and danger better than I otherwise should—and yet not so well." Ross, though fourteen years younger than Franklin, refused the command because of his age, and at the beginning of February, 1845, Franklin's appointment was confirmed.

The next three months were filled with the urgencies of preparation. As the time for departure drew near, Jane struggled harder and harder to control her feelings—to be brave and to appear confident at the parting. But there was uneasiness in her, and in Franklin, too. He feared that Eleanor, his daughter by his first marriage, might not, should anything happen to him, be of sufficient comfort to Jane. He therefore laid on his niece, Sophia Cracroft, the charge of staying with his wife until his return. As it turned out, for the next thirty years the two were hardly ever separated. Jane also had moments of uneasiness, and of fear more subtle than Sir John's. One day her husband, who had just had influenza, lay on a sofa, asleep; she sat near by, putting the last stitches to a flag for him to take north. Afraid that he might be feeling the cold, she hurriedly finished her work and threw the flag over his feet. At its touch, he half-woke and said: "Why, there's a flag thrown over me. Don't you know they lay the Union Jack over a corpse?" Jane turned pale and her heart sank; she had scarcely thought with her innocent act to bring forth so dark an omen. She tried to forget the incident, but could not; the best she could do was to hide her anxiety.

She buried herself in the last details of preparation: anything she could get for her husband or his shipmates, they should have. She put aboard the *Erebus* herself many small comforts and amusements, among them a backgammon board and a letter-nip. When she heard that the officers wanted a monkey, she hurried to provide it. On May 19 the vessels sailed. As the *Erebus* moved away from the pier, Franklin kept his eyes on Jane and repeatedly waved his handkerchief in affectionate farewell. Jane was struck by the sight of a dove that settled on one of the masts and moved out to sea with the ships. Could she have asked a finer omen of peace and harmony and good luck? She watched her husband's ship sail slowly down the Thames, and felt relief: the parting was over, and she had borne it well. A little later, in a letter directed to Franklin at the Orkneys, she wrote: "I wish we could see you in a glass as they do in the fairy-tales." It was a wish she was to have time and time again.

From Stromness Franklin answered her letter. His was more full of the expedition than of affection. Everybody was well and happy. The *Erebus* and the *Terror* sailed splendidly together; they would be good company-keepers. The Davis Strait men in the Orkneys said that the expedition was off in good time. The more he saw of Gore, the more convinced he was that he had a treasure and a faithful friend. Because of the weather, Crozier had not been aboard the *Erebus* much; when he did come, he was cheerful and happy. The mood of the letter was one of confidence and success; there was no need to worry about what lay ahead.

The next news would be from the Whalefish Islands, with the return of the transport *Barretto Junior*. This news was dreaded a little as being the last; but when, in the middle of

August, the letters came, they were surprisingly cheering. Franklin, in a sixteen-page letter brimming with hope, brought the story of the expedition up to date for Jane and mentioned his impatience to be on the way. Osmer, the purser on the *Erebus*, wrote his wife to expect him home in 1846. Other officers were equally optimistic. Fitzjames wrote that there was laughter from morning till night; and in his journal, which he sent back, there was an entry about the monkey. This entry, made by daylight at 10:30 in the evening of June 23 said: "The monkey has, however, just put on a blanket, frock, and trowsers, which the sailors have made him (or rather her), so I suppose it is getting cold." At the Whale-fish Islands the weather was fine; to the north the ice was supposed to be loose up to the 74th degree of latitude. With such good tidings, how could Jane help feeling relieved of her worst fears? Crozier, in a letter to James Clark Ross, struck the only sour note; he feared they might "blunder into the ice and make a second 1824 of it"—that being the year the *Fury* came to grief at Fury Beach in Prince Regent Inlet. But surely Ross had more sense than to pass this letter on to Lady Franklin.

Now the long wait began. Jane spent the summer of 1845 in France, the next summer sightseeing in America. Travel somehow refreshed her spirits and made it easier to bear the suspense. Also, in America, she was nearer her husband; even on the continent he was trying to circumnavigate. In August, 1846, she headed for home. That fall would most likely bring good news, and she wanted to be in England to get it. But no news came in October or November—the two months she had most counted on; and the year ended in disappointment.

The year 1847 was no better. Jane spent from April till

August in Italy. There, for her, the second anniversary of Franklin's sailing passed and though she was quite unaware of it, so did the date of his death—June 11. By September the government was considering plans for search parties—one to Bering Strait, one to the mouth of the Mackenzie and one to Lancaster Sound. None of these covered the spot where Jane thought her husband would be found—somewhere not far from the estuary of the Great Fish River, right along by King William Land itself. It was there, she was convinced, that as early a search as possible should be made. But the Admiralty, unfortunately, did not agree.

The next year, 1848, saw search parties started from England. In January the *Plover*, under Commander Moore, sailed for Bering Strait by way of Cape Horn to examine the arctic coast eastward to the mouth of the Mackenzie. If Franklin had almost, but not quite, made the passage, he would be found somewhere along there. In March Sir John Richardson and Dr. John Rae left for Canada to lead an overland party down the Mackenzie and from its mouth eastward to the Coppermine. Jane had wanted badly to go with Richardson, but in the end had given up the idea. Last, in May, Sir James Clark Ross, with the *Enterprise* and the *Investigator*, set out for Lancaster Sound. Ross carried with him a letter from Jane to her husband. "My dearest love," it began. "May it be the will of God if you are not restored to us earlier that you should open this letter & that it may give you comfort in all your trials. . . ." It was like sending a letter beyond the ends of the earth, so long would it take for an answer to come back. More than another year, at the least, must go by before Jane could even hear that her letter had reached her husband.

She still clung to her belief that Franklin would be found

146

near the mouth of the Great Fish River. She could not get it out of her head that he had followed his instructions to the letter and turned south or southwest from Barrow Strait. She was certain he had tried to reach the coast by the most direct route. Had he not, before he sailed, pointed on a map to the western end of Simpson Strait and remarked that if he could get there, his troubles would be over? By March, 1849, the Admiralty was concerned enough to offer a reward of twenty thousand pounds to any ship that brought help to the missing expedition. Yet that same Admiralty refused to look for Franklin in the place where he had said he was going. Worse, in May of 1849, they refused to sell Jane two dockyard lighters, which she wanted to outfit at her own expense and send out on a search. She accepted the rebuff with good grace; and in July she and Sophy left for the Orkneys and the Shetlands. Soon the whalers would be coming back from Baffin Bay, and one of them might bring news of her husband. She sensed that tragedy was closing in; but some word, even if it were bad, would be better than none. All that any whaler brought back in 1849 was a bottle picked up on the Greenland coast. In it was a paper from the *Erebus*, signed by Franklin and dated the 30th of June, 1845. On the paper was the ship's position and the message that all was well. Nothing could have been more disappointing; it was almost worse than nothing at all.

By October Jane and Sophy were back home, and in that month a strange thing happened in Londonderry. In the previous May a little Irish girl of four, Weesy Coppin, had died of gastric fever. Shortly after her death a presence that her brothers and sisters accepted as hers began to appear among them. Sometimes the presence was in the form of a blue light, again in little Weesy's own shape and likeness; oftenest the presence was just a strong feeling that she was among them. The children took the appearance perfectly for granted and every day set a place for Weesy at the table. She did not speak; instead she had her say by words that appeared in large letters on the wall. Soon she began to show amazing powers of revelation. One night, just at bedtime, she announced: "Mr. M'kay is dead." Mr. M'kay was a great friend of the children, and they all cried out against the announcement, but the next morning word came that the poor man had died in his sleep.

From time to time other demonstrations of Weesy's strange powers followed. One October evening, when Weesy was present as a blue light, the children's aunt asked one of Weesy's sisters to inquire about Sir John Franklin. The child did as she was asked. At once the blue light faded from sight, and the room grew cold as if from the chill of ice itself. The next minute "there appeared on the floor a complete Arctic scene, showing two ships, surrounded with ice and almost covered with snow, including a channel that led to the ships." There then " 'appeared' on the opposite wall, in large round hand letters, about three inches in length, the following:— '*Erebus* and *Terror*. Sir John Franklin, Lancaster Sound, Prince Regent Inlet, Point Victory, Victoria Channel.' "

Here, then, was a clue to where the ships were. The message made sense, and it fitted the chartlike scene that had appeared on the floor. The *Erebus* and the *Terror* were off the northwest coast of King William Land; they could be reached by going down Prince Regent Inlet and through the channel shown on the chart. The channel was the only questionable feature of the revelation; it was Bellot Strait, and in

1849 Bellot Strait had not been discovered. Captain Coppin, Weesy's father, communicated the story of the revelation to Lady Franklin and gave her a sketch, drawn by Weesy's sister, of the arctic scene. It was a strong confirmation of Lady Franklin's own view of where her husband was; it was bound to have its influence.

In November, within three days of each other, Richardson and Ross were back in England. Their news was equally bad. Richardson had found no sign of Franklin between the mouth of the Mackenzie and the mouth of the Coppermine. He had been able to pick up no word of Franklin from Indians on his route; if the expedition had passed along the coast, the Indians of the interior would have had at least hearsay information of it. He had left Rae at Fort Confidence to carry on the search on Victoria Land. Ross had done no better than Richardson. Ice conditions had been bad, and the *Enterprise* and *Investigator* had wintered at Port Leopold at the northeast corner of North Somerset. In the spring a party went to Fury Beach, only to find no word from Franklin there. Ross himself, accompanied by Leopold McClintock, sledged down the east side of Peel Sound almost to Bellot Strait. They were within sight of Cape Bird, which they named, when short rations and exhaustion forced them to turn back. Unknowing, they had stood about one hundred and eighty miles from where the *Erebus* and the *Terror* had been abandoned nearly a year before. Along the way they did not find a single trace of the expedition, and Ross concluded that the ships could not have taken that route and that he, himself, was the discoverer of Peel Sound. It was all sad news for Jane. Although neither Ross nor Richardson had reached the spot she would have chosen, she had hoped for something tangible from the searches. Even an empty meat tin or a part of a sledge or a faded note from a cairn would have brought her some comfort, given her some encouragement. Instead she had nothing at all; for a time she had hardly the will to carry on.

By the end of 1849 four and a half years had gone by since Franklin sailed. The party could still be eking out their three years' provisions, if the provisions had been added to by game and fish. But the margin of safety was growing thinner every day; help, if it were going to reach the expedition in time, could not wait long. In 1850 an all-out effort was made. It was hide-and-seek played too well by the hider—a guessing game with too many guesses possible. If the *Erebus* and the *Terror* had not gone down Peel Sound and had not been seen by natives along the coast, then, quite obviously, they were not in the region southwest of Lancaster Sound. The Admiralty's next guess was that they had been caught in the ice near Melville Island or west of it—this despite the fact that Franklin had been warned to avoid that ice at all costs. Parry, in 1819-20, had seen great herds of musk oxen on Melville Island; it was possible the Franklin men had retreated to Melville for fresh meat. Wellington Channel, of course, was another waterway they might have entered in their search for a Northwest Passage; it could not be overlooked. Slowly the searches turned the wrong way; to the south only Rae was left, pursuing the search on Victoria Land.

In January 1850 the *Enterprise* and the *Investigator*, under Captain Collinson and Captain McClure, sailed for Bering Strait by way of Cape Horn, to try to reach Melville Island from the west. In April the *Lady Franklin*, her figurehead a feminine Hope, and the *Sophia*, under Captain Penny, sailed for Wellington Channel. A week after the *Lady Franklin* and the *Sophia* had left England, the *Felix* and the *Mary* sailed, bound for Banks Land. The *Felix* and *Mary* expedition was financed mainly by the Hudson's Bay Company; in command was old Sir John Ross, of *Victory* fame, now seventy-three. In May two more expeditions left their home ports. One was a large British expedition of four ships, under Captain Austin. He was to sail to Lancaster Sound and into the waters west, and to send out sledge expeditions to Melville Island and the coasts in the neighborhood of Cape Walker. The other was an American expedition of two ships; it sailed from New York for Barrow Strait, Wellington Channel, and other likely points north or west. By the end of May twelve ships were on their way north to search for the Franklin party; each ship was headed for a wrong spot.

Jane had her own—and different—plan. She was going to send an expedition to the right spot, even should such an expedition take her last penny. She had by now another argument for searching near the mouth of the Great Fish River. When her husband sailed, some geographers thought Boothia and North Somerset were an island, and that James Ross Strait ran into the bottom of Prince Regent Inlet. If Franklin shared this opinion, might he not have sailed down Prince Regent Inlet into Ross Strait and there been caught in the ice? If such had been the event, he would probably then have abandoned his ships and made for the Great Fish River. Jane's expedition would sail down Prince Regent Inlet to the narrowest point of North Somerset. From there sledge parties would cross over to the west side of Somerset and turn south down the coast of Boothia. If these parties did not come upon the *Erebus* and the *Terror*, they might hear word of them from the Eskimos.

From the beginning of the year 1850 Jane worked furiously. The only suitable sailing ship that fitted her purse was a tiny ninety-ton ex-pilot boat, the *Prince Albert*. She bought it and, with the help of friends, fitted it out, supervising the work herself. In command she put Captain Charles C. Forsyth, a naval man who had volunteered his services; unfortunately, he had had no experience in arctic navigation. The chief mate did not know how to use a chronometer and could neither write nor spell well enough to keep a log. The second mate's one joy was to think and act in opposition to his chief. By far the most curious character aboard was William Parker Snow, second in command, "long used"—in his own words—"to a rough and wandering life." Obsessed with the idea of finding Franklin, he had come from Canada to join the *Lady Franklin* under Penny. The *Lady Franklin* had already sailed; if Snow wanted to get in on the search at all, he would have to join the *Prince Albert* expedition. By the time the *Prince Albert* sailed Snow was the ship's doctor. The official doctor had arrived from Glasgow two days before the sailing date, taken one look at the tiny vessel, and politely bowed out. Snow fearlessly stepped into the breach. As he put it, "Medicine had to me long been a pleasing study . . . With M'Arthur's excellent little book of directions, Reece's invaluable Medical Guide, and the humble skill I myself possessed I thought all would be well." There is no record of the thoughts of the seventeen other men aboard.

The *Prince Albert* sailed from Aberdeen on June 5, late in the year, but unavoidably so; it was the earliest the ship could be got ready. On the eve of the sailing Lady Franklin confided to Snow the details of Weesy Coppin's revelation. Also, and much less romantically, she confided to his care an ear trumpet; her husband was deaf, and the trumpet might prove handy in talking to him. All through the day of sailing the quay swarmed with relatives and well-wishers and the curious. At six o'clock Captain Forsyth arrived, and by eight o'clock the little vessel was off. Jane was missing from the dockside crowd; she had spared herself the strain of seeing her own expedition leave.

In the early stages of the voyage the little ship had more luck than was hoped for. She made a fast crossing of the North Atlantic and by July 11 was off the Whalefish Islands; ten days later she had caught up with the *Felix*, Sir John Ross's ship, which had left England on April 20. The ice was unusually heavy in Baffin Bay, and the other search ships were still battering and ramming and dynamiting their way through. On the last day of the month the *Prince Albert* was eight miles from Austin's armada, and soon, near the famous crimson cliffs north of Cape York, nine of the British ships engaged in the Franklin search from the east were together. Probably never in history have so many explorers with their ships gathered in one place. The *Prince Albert* was now the gainer from her late start. First one of Austin's steamers, then the other, took her in tow, and thus assisted she got quickly through the heaviest of the pack. Once in the clear waters beyond Melville Bay, she fairly flew along. Snow, filled with romantic dreams, likened the expedition to that of Baffin in the 55-ton *Discovery*. On August 20 the *Prince Albert* entered Lancaster Sound, and the next morning, at 2:30, they were off Port Leopold, the first of the search ships to arrive in Barrow Strait.

Snow could not wait to get ashore. It was at Port Leopold that Ross, with the *Enterprise* and the *Investigator*, had spent the winter of 1848-49. He had left there a house and supplies and a launch, on the chance that some part of the Franklin expedition, perhaps trying to make its way to the whaling fleet, might come upon them. If any of Franklin's men had visited the spot, there would be a message. The *Prince Albert's* gutta-percha boat was launched, and Snow and a party rowed to shore. They found the house still standing and a quantity of supplies still on the beach, but no word from the lost expedition. In a few hours they were back on the ship, which now headed down Prince Regent Inlet.

The wind was light and the weather too thick to see far ahead; the little ship crept along, past Elwin Bay and on southward. Toward evening they passed Batty Bay; the fog hung on, and heavy ice stretched out farther and farther from the shore. At seven the next morning they were off Fury Beach; in a little under twenty-four hours they had come only eighty-five miles. Visibility continued bad; it was hard to get any picture of what lay about them. At nine the fog lifted; abeam lay the coast, trending to the west, and in every direction ahead, and on all sides, there was nothing but ice. Snow, with his spyglass, mounted to the crow's nest, but "nothing save one dreary expanse of heavy hummocky stuff presented itself. Not a sign of any opening anywhere." What was more, the ship had run into a bight; if a gale or even breezy weather came up, she might be nipped.

The chief mate was called from his bed and sent aloft; the second mate took one of the ship's boats to try the pack. For once the two men agreed: it would be impossible for the ship to go farther into the ice that season. Forsyth ordered the ship's head brought around, and the *Prince Albert* began to retrace her course northward, away from the relics that awaited discovery on King William Land.

The expedition had failed of its purpose. It could not go back and completely disappoint Lady Franklin. It would try somewhere else. Ice filled Barrow Strait to the west: Cape Walker could not be reached. There was left, then, the possibility of Wellington Channel. The other search ships were already converging on this area, and again the *Prince Albert* found herself in company. She passed by Beechey Island and turned up the east side of Wellington Channel. Only a few miles in, ice stopped her, and she had to turn back. She swung eastward around Beechey Island and was off Cape Riley when she sighted, in the same moment, the *Advance*, one of the American ships, close in shore, and beyond the *Advance*, on the tip of the cape, a signal post. The signal could mean nothing but important news. At once Snow and a party were off in the ship's boat. He boarded the *Advance* and learned from Captain De Haven that "traces" had been found ashore, and that the whole story of the find was in a dispatch at the signal post. Soon Snow was at the post itself. The dispatch was concise and to the point. It stated that "Captain Ommanney, with the officers of her Majesty's ships *Assistance* and *Intrepid*, landed at Cape Riley on the 23rd of August, 1850, where he found traces of an encampment, and collected the remains of materials which evidently prove that some party belonging to her Majesty's ships have been detained on this spot. Beechey Island was also examined, where traces were found of the same party." The date of the dispatch was two days before

Snow's arrival; at the time the note was writen, the graves on Beechey Island and the ruins of the forge and the observatory and the storehouse had not yet been discovered.

Snow at once began a search of Cape Riley and found a piece of bleached canvas, an inch and a half square; a piece of 1½-inch rope, forty-four feet long; and beef and mutton bones. For Snow these were sufficient; he would not have to go back to Lady Franklin empty-handed. That very evening the *Prince Albert* sailed for home, and on October 1 she was in England again.

Had the *Prince Albert* delayed in the North, she could have brought back the full story of Franklin's first winter. A week after she left, the graves and ruins of various houses on Beechey Island had been found; also what was left of the garden, a cairn built of empty meat tins, the men's washtubs, even "a pair of Cashmere gloves laid out to dry, with two small stones on the palms to prevent their blowing away." On the high ridge at the southern end of the island the searchers came across a stone cairn, obviously built by the men of the expedition. But no note was found in it, no word of what direction the *Erebus* and the *Terror* had taken.

During the winter of 1850-51 many of the ships stayed in Barrow Strait, to be ready to continue the search with sledge parties in the spring. They tried in every possible way to communicate with the Franklin men—by kites, by balloons, by rockets and, more ingenious still, by messages stamped on copper collars, which were then put around wild foxes' necks. In the spring of 1851 two sledge parties set out for Cape Walker to search the coast of Prince of Wales Land, and a third party, under McClintock, who had been with Ross down the eastern shore of Peel Sound in 1849, made for the southern shore of Melville Island. No matter where the quest turned, it failed. In August the ships were blasted out of the ice with dynamite and set sail for home.

Jane had not been dismayed by the return of the *Prince Albert*; her heart was still set on the estuary of the Great Fish River. If the *Prince Albert* had failed once, that was nothing; she would send the ship out again.

She hoped to get it off in March, 1851, but it was June before the ship sailed—the only search party to leave that year. It bore all the marks of Jane's idealism; there was a curious unworldliness about it. In command was a generous-minded, good-natured Canadian, William Kennedy, who had volunteered for the job. He had had hardly any experience at sea, but he was so honest and so earnest and so hopeful that it seemed, at least to Jane, that he might win through. He wanted no glory or reward for himself, just the chance to rescue Franklin. Second in command was Lieutenant Bellot, a twenty-five-year-old French citizen, hardly less dedicated to the cause than his commander. He was chivalrous and a dreamer, with a lively interest in Franklin's fate. Jane liked him on first sight, and thereafter treated him as her "French son." At the time, many of her advisers held no high opinion of the French among ice, but in Bellot's case an exception was always made. Also aboard was old John Hepburn, the midshipman who had served under Franklin in Canada in 1820, when Franklin's whole party nearly starved to death crossing the Barren Lands. Now Hepburn was bent on saving his one-time commander. He was a little old, of course—sixty-two— and a little on the sentimental side; but what an addition he was to such a crew as was sailing—the old servant going out in search of his master, and signed on as supercargo. The sailing master was a veteran whaling captain; the doctor this time was a real one; and four of the crew had been with the *Prince Albert* the year before. In all there were eighteen men aboard, most of them chosen by Lady Franklin herself.

The ship was to be a temperance ship—"to sail," as Kennedy put it, "under cold water colors." She carried an organ, a gift from her namesake; it had originally been destined for the first expedition, but had not been delivered in time to sail. Seven carrier pigeons were taken, with explicit instructions for their release. "Lady Ross," the queen of the seven, was to be sent back only if Sir John himself were found alive; and if so sent, she was to be carefully marked on her breast with a red or black cross and the number "7" to show she had not escaped. She was a pigeon of no small accomplishments, having once already flown from Lancaster Sound to her home in Scotland. A tin kayak was carried, too. Kennedy had had some experience with the true Eskimo craft in Labrador, and he thought a metal one might prove handy. While preparations were under way, Weesy's "ice scenes" miraculously began again—perhaps a sign that the ship was headed for the right spot. Kennedy went to Londonderry to see the Coppins and came away much impressed by the revelations.

The *Prince Albert* left Stromness on June 3. Jane and Sophy went to the Orkneys to take care of the last-minute details and see the ship off. Kennedy's instructions were much the same as Forsyth's—to go down Prince Regent Inlet, cross North Somerset at its narrowest, then turn south. If a wife's intuition were right—to say nothing of Weesy's revelation— south of Lancaster Sound Franklin would be found. He had been gone over five years, but he might still be alive, particularly if he had fallen in with friendly natives. At two in the afternoon the little ship sailed away, her flags flying, her shrouds bedecked with "a lovely garland woven by the fair hands of the ladies of Stromness and Wolverhampton." During the hustle and bustle of getting off, one of the pigeons, quite unnoticed, had escaped. Two hours later she came back to the ship and settled in the rigging. Somehow she had reversed her homing instinct and rejoined her companions for the voyage north.

On September 4 the *Prince Albert* was off Port Leopold, in search of a likely spot to winter. Port Leopold was closed by ice. A run down the west side of Prince Regent Inlet showed Elwin Bay, Batty Bay and Fury Beach closed, too. Next Kennedy tried the east side of the inlet; Port Bowen was clear. In an emergency he could use it, but he decided to hold it for a last choice; all his work lay on the opposite side of the inlet. Once more the ship headed for Port Leopold; the ice that had closed it might have broken up. On September 9, at 7:00 P.M., the ship lay two miles off Cape Seppings, the southern arm of Port Leopold. A narrow lane of water seemed to lead to shore, and Kennedy and four men followed it in the gutta-percha boat. They found the harbor clear and satisfied themselves that the chances of getting the ship in to the harbor were good. They headed their little boat back for the ship, only to find their way blocked; a north wind had come up and "nothing could be seen or heard around us but huge masses of ice, grinding, tossing, and rearing furiously on every side." The gutta-percha boat was no match for such conditions; their only hope lay in regaining the shore. Two miles south of Cape Seppings they succeeded in beaching the boat, and there, in frozen clothes, they spent a miserable night, the upturned boat their only shelter. At dawn they hurried to the top of the cliff that rises beyond the beach. Not a sign of the *Prince Albert* was to be seen.

Fortunately, they had the house and the launch, the supplies and provisions left by Ross in 1849. The canvas walls of the house were rotted and torn away; it was much cozier to take up residence in the launch. At her bow and stern they built two supports, nine feet high, to hold her mainmast, laid horizontally; over the mast they spread two of her sails to make a tent. A stove was set up in the body of the boat, with pipes running through the tent roof; bags and blankets from the depot kept the men warm at night.

By the end of September they had abandoned hope that the *Prince Albert* would make her way back to them and had begun preparations for a sledging expedition to seek her out as soon as the ice was solid enough for traveling. The men set to work to make shoes from the canvas housing of the building, and the carpenter prepared wood for snowshoes and a winter sleigh. The first half of October passed uneventfully; the men grew more and more used to their quarters and to the possibility of having to spend the entire winter there. On October 17 a shot was heard outside the camp. Kennedy stepped out of the tent and saw Bellot and seven men. They had dragged the jolly boat all the way from Batty Bay, where the *Prince Albert* was safely moored for the winter. Twice before Bellot had tried to reach the beleaguered men. Now, on the third attempt, he had got through.

It took five days to pack up; then, thirteen men in all, the party headed back for the ship. "Our provisions and 'traps' of all kinds," Kennedy wrote, "were stowed in the boat, and the whole secured on a strong sleigh. A mast was then set, and a sail hoisted in the jolly boat, and away we went before a spanking fair wind over the smooth ice of Leopold harbor, at a rate which 'all the king's horses' could hardly have been equal to." That night they slept in a tiny tent—six of them sitting up on each side, with Bellot, the most stowable, tucked away under the assembled legs. All the next day they traveled, and the following day they were safely back at Batty Bay.

Immediately work was begun to get the ship ready for winter. Part of the stores were taken out of the hold and piled high on the ice. The decks were housed over with canvas and, except for a narrow entrance passage nearly amidships, the whole vessel was banked right up to the gunwales with snow. The outside work done, the men busied themselves making moccasins and warm clothing, snowshoes and dog-sleighs— everything that would be needed on their winter journeys. Their "conjuror," a sort of traveling cookstove that burned spirits of wine, had screws that could only be adjusted by the naked hand, not a happy arrangement in sub-zero weather. To take its place they devised an open hexagonal-shaped dish, with grooves at the corners for wicks. It worked well, giving an even, continuous flame. They hunted foxes and ptarmigan and sampled fox pie, which some found good and others likened to dead cats. Christmas day was fine and calm. For that day a shooting match had been arranged; "but the darkness was so great, that to avoid the risk of shooting each other, the match had to be put off." A football game was substituted, and the day "closed with some very dull speeches from the commander downwards. . . ."

On January 5 Kennedy and Bellot and three others set out for Fury Beach. No search party had been there since 1849; in the meantime a message might have been left. Their path led along the foot of high cliffs, over a boulder-strewn shore;

it was hard, by moonlight, to pick their way. Fury Beach itself was an eerie spot. "I stood paralyzed at the death-like solitude around us," wrote Kennedy. "No vestige of the visit of a human being was here since Lieut. Robinson had examined the depôt in 1849." The frame of Somerset House was still standing, but the gales had torn the canvas covering to shreds. The men lighted a fire in the stove and settled down to sample the stores, which still lay in neat piles on the beach. Everything was frozen but still good; in thirty years the vegetables had lost none of their taste. The party rested in Somerset House until midnight, then started the return journey; by January 12 they were at the ship again.

During the next six weeks depots were laid down between the ship and Fury Beach, the starting point of the search southward to the area where Lady Franklin believed her husband would be found. Kennedy's spirits rose and fell; his plans followed suit, now expanding, now shrinking. At one time he would go to Cape Bird, Cape Felix, Franklin Point, Montreal Island, Pelly Bay, Felix Harbour; then back up the east coast of Boothia. Three weeks later the plan had shrunk; he would go on foot no farther than the Magnetic Pole, return to Batty Bay, and end the journey by taking boats down to Brentford Bay and launching them on the lake of Boothia—just what for he never made clear. The truth was, the unknown lay ahead and no plan could cover what they might encounter.

A first detachment left for Fury Beach on February 25. It took nine days to get there; the weather was bad and the going rough all the way. When they arrived their canvas moccasins and snowshoes and sleighs were so damaged as to need making over from scratch. A second detachment, or fatigue party, joined the first at Fury Beach on March 7. Somerset House was made as livable as possible, and the men settled down to repair their equipment; a group went back to the ship for supplies. At 9:00 A.M. on March 29, with the temperature 26° below zero, the southern journey began. Lady Franklin's instructions were at last to be carried out.

In the party were Kennedy and Bellot and twelve men and five dogs; with them was a ton of equipment, neatly lashed to four flat-bottomed Indian sleighs. Some of the men wore cloth masks to protect their faces against the frost; others muffled themselves up in chin-cloths and wore gutta-percha noses. These noses, lined with soft flannel, were a great success until taken off, when most of the skin came off too. Kennedy's final plan was for the whole party to go to Brentford Bay, where North Somerset was supposed to be at its narrowest. The fatigue party would then return, and Kennedy and Bellot and six men would cross the isthmus and go down the west coast to the Magnetic Pole. What they did after that would depend on their condition and whether they had picked up any word of Franklin or his men.

They made eighteen miles the first day, and slept that night in an enormous snow house that fell down twice in the making and took nearly five hours to build. As they went southward the weather grew milder and the coast flattened. The third day out they were at Cresswell Bay. The next day they came upon the remains of twenty Eskimo huts; considerably farther on, they saw the footprints of an Eskimo man and child; but they met no natives. At the end of a week they entered Brentford Bay and struck for Brown's Island, where John Ross had been in 1829. From the island's northern side they looked into the entrance of an inlet extending westward off Brentford Bay as far as they could see. A thick cloud of mist was rising from this inlet, suggesting open water; there were lofty granite cliffs on either side. Was it possible that Weesy Coppin had been right? Was there an actual channel from Prince Regent Inlet to the Western Sea? It was too late in the day to investigate; darkness was coming on.

The next day, April 6, was fine, with a morning temperature of −13°. At eight o'clock the fatigue party left to return to the ship. Kennedy and Bellot and four men stayed behind. They had the five dogs and two sleighs and 600 pounds of provisions. "Besides this," wrote Bellot, "we have each a blanket, a buffalo-robe between two, a macintosh cloth, the sextant, the air-boat, the things for barter with the Esquimaux, three guns and their ammunition, and twenty pair of moccasins: we carry upon us all the body linen we are to use during the journey." They did not start on their travels at once, but first spent a day examining Brentford Bay, Bellot going southward and Kennedy in the direction of the column of mist they had seen the evening before. Just as he expected, it rose from open water—a mile or more of it—in a wide channel leading to the west. Four miles farther on he came to more open water. Here there was so strong a current that blocks of ice were drifting along at nearly five miles an hour. Kennedy climbed a nearby hill and saw in the distance a sea stretching westward, with the strait apparently running into it. There could be no doubt about Weesy's "ice scene" now; this strait he was in was the channel it showed.

On April 7 the party was on its way. All day they traveled westward along what is now Bellot Strait. The weather was cold and clear, 25° below in the morning and 16° below at noon, with a biting wind from the west. Along the way they saw the recent tracks of innumerable caribou and musk oxen. At six in the evening, after more than twenty miles of traveling, they came to the western end of the strait and made camp. Cape Felix and the key to the Franklin mystery lay barely 150 miles to the south. So far the search party had followed Lady Franklin's instructions to the letter; one more turn in the right direction, and the party would be headed directly for its goal.

This turn Kennedy never took. He looked to the north and thought he saw a barrier of land from North Somerset across to what is now Prince of Wales Island. Peel Sound, he then reasoned, was only a gulf, not a passageway Franklin could have sailed through to the south. Perhaps farther west there was another channel Franklin had taken; better to continue in that direction and look for it. Thus Kennedy missed his chance.

The next day, April 8, the little party continued west. Two days later they reached Prince of Wales Island, Kennedy still convinced that Peel Sound had no navigable outlet to the south. He crossed Prince of Wales Island to Ommanney Bay, then returned to the east coast of the island and followed it north to Cape Walker, which he reached on May 4. From there he crossed the ice to North Somerset and on May 30 was back at the ship. He had been gone ninety-seven days on a futile journey of 1,100 miles. On August 6 the *Prince Albert* got free of the ice and sailed away from Batty Bay.

On the homeward voyage, off Cape Riley, the vessel fell in with the *North Star*, one of the five ships, under Sir Edward Belcher, sent out in the spring of 1852 to search for Franklin north of Beechey Island, up Wellington Channel; then, if no sign of him had been found, westward along the

northern shores of Cornwallis and Bathurst and Melville islands. Since the return of the 1850 parties, with their report
of failure to find any sign of Franklin either west or south of
Beechey Island, the Admiralty had been convinced that
Franklin, after spending his first winter on Beechey Island,
had sailed north. It was in that direction that they were making a last effort to find him. By the *North Star* Kennedy received a letter from Lady Franklin, requesting him and his
ship to join Belcher's expedition. Kennedy and Bellot were
anxious to do so, but the crew objected, and the *Prince Albert*
continued on her way home. She reached Aberdeen October
7, 1852.

For a second time Jane was not dismayed by the failure of
the *Prince Albert* to bring news of her husband. During the
sixteen months that the little ship had been gone, she, too,
had wavered in her conviction of where her husband would
be found. Perhaps, after all, he had gone not south from
Beechey Island but north, possibly across the top of the world
to the neighborhood of Bering Strait or the Siberian coast. As
far back as October 1851—four months after the *Prince Albert* had sailed—Jane had tried to organize an expedition to
go through Bering Strait and search eastward; but her plans,
after the purchase of a ship, the *Isabel,* fell through. In April
1853—six months after the *Prince Albert's* return—the *Isabel*
sailed for the New Siberian Islands, the expedition this time
financed by the colonists of Van Diemen's land and commanded by Captain Kennedy. At Valparaiso the crew deserted
and the enterprise came to an end.

Jane now pinned her hopes on Belcher's expedition. A
month after the *Isabel's* departure the Admiralty sent two
ships to Beechey Island to deposit supplies for Belcher. They

reached the island in August and returned home with the news that not a trace of Franklin had been found. His expedition had now been gone eight and a half years; it was still a complete mystery where the *Erebus* and the *Terror* had gone after leaving Beechey Island. By this late date all the Franklin men were surely dead. The Admiralty decided to risk no further lives in what seemed so hopeless a cause. As soon as a ship could be got to Belcher the next summer, he would be recalled.

On January 12, 1854 Jane received word that on March 31, unless good news of some kind were received before then, the names of the officers and men of the *Erebus* and the *Terror* would be removed from the books of the Admiralty; the members of the Franklin expedition would be considered to have died in Her Majesty's service.

To Jane this meant but one thing: the abandonment by the Admiralty of all hope of ever finding her husband. To them he was gone forever, and with him all his men and his two ships. The blow crushed her; for a week she could not even take up pen to reply. She then refused to claim her widow's pension. And in a protest pathetic in its defiant bravery, she changed to bright colors from the mourning she had been wearing for years.

4.

While the outside world wondered about the Franklin expedition, life on Kikerktak went on with little change.
It was a pattern of life that the people of Kikerktak had to
follow closely if they were to have shelter, clothing, and food.
There was the autumn caribou hunt at Malerualik, the winter
sealing on the sea ice, the spring caribou hunt at the crossing
places on the lakes and rivers, and the August fishing at
Amitsoq, the place where the spirits felt kindly toward man.
Now when the Kikerktarmiut gathered at Amitsoq with their
friends from afar—friends from Boothia and from Adelaide
Peninsula—strange stories were told of the white men who
had come to Kikerktak only to die.

First was the story of the meeting at Cape Herschel. Had
not Owwer and Tutkeeta and Monger and Tooshooarthariu
and their families actually seen the white men and talked with
them? They had not understood all that the white men told
them; they had taken in little more than that the strangers had
left their ships in the ice and were on their way to the mainland to hunt caribou. But when it came to what the white
men looked like, no detail had been missed. All except one

were terribly thin—*ooksook* (i.e. fat) all gone. One man was short with a narrow face and a big nose. Another was tall but did not laugh or smile. A third had sore, bleeding lower gums; many had bleeding lips—probably, the natives thought, from eating too much snow. There was a man with a red beard and a man with gray hair and a man with an upper tooth missing. All the men's clothing was dark, and the top part came down almost to the knees; everything about the strangers was different. They had a big boat on a big sledge and a smaller sledge with camp things on it. They took seal meat that did not belong to them; they fished for salmon and made birds drop out of the sky. Some of them went to bed in the boat and some in a big white tent.

It was a wonderful meeting with strange people, and made a story to be told over and over again. Part of its fascination was that there was always something in the story to be a little afraid of. When Tutkeeta had first seen the white men's boat out on the ice he had thought it a bear. Then he and his companions saw dark objects moving along with the white object; it was quite near when they made out that the white object was a boat with its sail up, and the dark objects men—strangers—who were drawing the boat. One could never be sure with strangers; that was why Owwer and Tooshoo-arthariu, when they went out to meet the men, stopped at the widest crack in the ice they could find. There was the same uneasiness in the end of the story. Perhaps the people of the island should have stayed longer with the white men; but one has one's own people to think of. Decidedly, the story of the meeting at Cape Herschel was one to be told many times before everything in it could be understood.

Then there was the story of the tent near Toonoonee, as the

part of Kikerktak around Terror Bay was called. Tutkeeta and his brother Tennea and a third man Etkerlit found it in the spring, about a year after the meeting between Tutkeeta and the white men. Snow and ice had crushed the tent partly down, and a fox had bitten one of the lines in two. Close by was a place on the ground where another big tent must have stood; probably, Tutkeeta thought, the white men he met near Cape Herschel had once camped here. There were three graves, the earth above them raised in long, narrow mounds. Tutkeeta and Tennea and Etkerlit looked all around the place where the white men had been, then went back to their own camping place with the news of what they had found. At once all their people—men, women and children—hurried to the tent.

Inside was a horrible sight—blankets and bedding and the bodies of a great many white men, some with the flesh still on, others with the flesh all gone, as if foxes and wolves had been gnawing at them. Scattered everywhere were the things that white men carry with them: cups, spoons, knives, forks, guns and powder flasks. There were also books and papers, but these no one had any use for; they threw them away, except one book with pictures, which Tutkeeta took home for his children. There was a box with compartments, and in the compartments things with strong smells. What the things were no one knew, but the smell could never be forgotten. Above all, there were a great many shining things, watches and their chains, some still around the wearers' necks. In time word of what had been discovered in the tent spread afar; other natives came to see what they could find.

One day a woman, standing among the frozen corpses, saw the body of a man lying on its side, half embedded in ice. The man looked more asleep than dead, as if he had died all alone.

Around his neck was a chain that ran down into the ice that his body was frozen to. The woman knew what was at the end of the chain; she had seen other women with objects like it. Now she wanted the watch and chain more than anything else in the world. How to get them was another thing; she had with her no tool for chopping away the ice. While her husband looked about the tent for objects that would catch his fancy, the woman picked up a sharp stone and set to work. As she chipped the ice from the man's face, she felt uneasy, and many times she had to stop. But she went on with the job, always careful not to let the stone touch the flesh. At last she finished her work, and her husband helped her lift the man from his icy bed. Then the watch and the chain and the key became hers. Never had she forgotten the feeling she had when she dug the dead Kabloona out of the ice with nothing but a sharp stone. Such, then, was what happened in the tent near Toonoonee, when it was visited by the Kikerktarmiut.

There were stories, too, of bodies found along the island's southern shore, buried in a strange way, faces up and the hands carefully folded across the breasts, the graves made by placing stones around and over the bodies. Neewikkeei found the first two in the spring, about a year after the men had died; they were just east of the Peffer River. The bodies were perfect, with all the clothes still on, and in each grave was a knife. Neewikkeei felt sorry the men had died with no one who knew the land to help them, but how wonderful it was to find knives! Near were lines of stones that had held down a big, four-sided tent. Scattered on the ground were the bones of the fish the white men had caught and eaten. There were many, many needles and one nail.

Also told was the story of the body found on Kungearklearu —the long low spit of land that runs out into Simpson Strait at James Ross Point. Just like the two bodies near the Peffer River, this body was perfectly preserved and had all its clothes on. It was the body of a large, tall man, and there was something horrible about the gums of his lower jaw: they were dry and hard and black. The man must have been terribly sick. One of the men seen by Owwer and Tutkeeta near Cape Herschel had had the same kind of bad lower gums. Just what his mouth looked like had been told over and over again: it was a kind of sight not seen among the Kikerktarmiut. Perhaps the man on Kungearklearu and the man at Cape Herschel were the same man. Not far from his body, when he was found at Kungearklearu, were a spyglass and two spoons wrapped in a blanket.

That same spring a man named Pooyetta, who had been on Ross's *Victory* nineteen years before, found five bodies on Keeuna. The bodies were not buried, but were lying close together on top of the ground on a high part of the island. All the flesh was on the bones; each body was fully dressed in dark clothes. There was a knife in one man's pocket; near another man, who lay a little apart from the rest, was an unopened tin can. Pooyetta opened it and found it full of meat with lots of fat in it, all still good to eat; it was the kind of food white men brought with them in their ships.

It was at the inlet on the west side of Richardson Point that Pooyetta made his most amazing find. Friends were with him at the time, and also his wife and twelve-year-old son. At the bottom of the inlet they came to a cove, around which the land was so flat and low that with snow still on it, it seemed almost a part of the frozen sea. Drawn up on the shore of the cove was a boat, standing on its keel and quite undamaged. Pooyetta was certain it was the same boat that the white men had with them near Cape Herschel. On the ground nearby were a number of skulls, some arm bones and leg bones, and a keg of black sand stuff (gunpowder), much of it spilled out on the beach. A canvas awning covered the boat from end to end. When Pooyetta looked inside, he saw many bodies under blankets, as if they were in bed. Some of them did not look long dead. They might have died the winter before. Pooyetta saw guns, gold and silver watches, and a big tin box, also a pair of gold spectacles and some wire snow goggles. These things Pooyetta knew about, for he had seen other things like them brought to his land by white men. There was a red tin full of tobacco and some pipes, probably treasured by the dying men till the last. On the finger of one dead man was a ring, which was taken off and given to the children to play with. From the other treasures lying about, Pooyetta and his friends took what they wanted. Eventually, the boat was broken up for the precious wood that was in it.

Pooyetta came away from the place with strange tales to tell. The dead man with the ring on his finger had a gold watch chain so tangled around his ears that by pulling on it the whole head could be lifted up. The effect was laughable, but frightening, too; it was almost as if the man had suddenly come to life. Pooyetta's son and a playmate found a canister with some black sand stuff in it—the same kind of stuff that was in the keg. The children took the canister into the snow house to play with. Somehow they managed to start the gunpowder burning, whereupon there was a terrific explosion, and the snow house was blown to pieces. The fire burned and blackened the children's faces; no one was killed. Nothing like this explosion had ever happened before, and the story of it was always told with the other stories about the boat and the dead men that were found in the inlet to the west of Richardson Point.

The other story that was told and told again was of the great ship that sank off Ookjoolik, the west side of Adelaide Peninsula, the same spring that the tent and the boat were found. Nukkeecheuk and some friends, when they were out sealing, looked to the northeast and saw a ship frozen in the ice. At the sight of it they were very much afraid, and all but Nukkeecheuk went back to the snow houses. Nukkeecheuk took courage and went toward the ship, which was big, with three masts, and had boats hanging at its sides, and the deck covered over with heavy cloth to make a kind of tent. The ice about the ship was of the winter's making—all smooth; and on it were scrapings and sweepings, as if someone had been, or still was, living on the ship. A gangway was in place. To Nukkeecheuk everything looked in good order. He listened and watched, but saw no one and heard nothing. Then he went on board and picked up a few things, among them a knife, and hurried back with them to the camp. When the others heard what Nukkeecheuk said and saw what he had found, they, too, went to the ship. They broke into a place that was fastened up, and there on the floor lay a big, dead white man, his remains perfect and fully clothed. The place smelt very bad. It took five men to lift up the body; they did not carry it anywhere, just put it back down again where it was. In the ship were treasures of every kind—knives, spoons, forks, pans, cups and plates; guns and boxes and buckets and casks. There were bright-colored red tins, some empty and others full of meat mixed with plenty of fat. Everywhere they looked, their eyes fell on strange and puzzling things, unlike anything they had ever seen before. Inside the ship it was so dark they had to feel their way around and carry out into the light the things they came on. One side of the ship had been damaged by the ice; they were able to wrench out broken timbers and get directly inside her. Everything they could possibly want was theirs for the taking.

Whenever they could, they want back to the vessel and pillaged her from end to end. A few things they carried away with them, but most of their loot they piled high on the deck; when all they wanted was on the deck, they would come back for it with sledges. The day came to take their riches off the ship, and they set forth from their camp in high spirits. They drew near the ship, but not a sign of her could they see. On getting close, they saw her masts sticking out of the water. The ship had sunk, and down with the ship had gone all their treasure. In time storms and ice broke up the vessel, and masts and timbers and wreckage of all kinds floated ashore on the coast of Ookjoolik.

Not long after the sinking of the ship, the tracks of four white men and a dog were seen in the snow on the mainland. There was no mistaking the tracks of the men; they were long and thin in the middle—the kind of tracks only white men's boots make. Those who had seen the tracks thought one of the white men must have been a great runner; his steps were unusually long. The tracks went on for some distance to a place where a young caribou had been killed and eaten. The men themselves were never seen.

These, then, were the stories told at Amitsoq about the white men who came to Kikerktak in two ships. One ship foundered off Ookjoolik; the other, so a story went, was seen to sink in deep water off the island's western coast. Most of the men died on their way to the Great Fish River. All this, and probably more, the Kikerktarmiut knew. They wondered endlessly where the ships had come from and what the white men were seeking in the North. But where the lost expedition had gone was no puzzle to them at all.

5.

On April 21, 1854—just twenty-one days after the Admiralty had removed from its books the names of the officers and men of the *Erebus* and *Terror*—the unraveling of the mystery of the Franklin expedition began. Dr. John Rae, under Hudson's Bay Company orders, was on his way from Repulse Bay to the western coast of Boothia to chart the unexplored gaps between Dease and Simpson's cairn at the Castor and Pollux River and the western entrance to Bellot Strait. Already, in 1847, Rae had filled in the blank stretch around the southern end of the Gulf of Boothia, from Ross's Lord Mayor's Bay to Fury and Hecla Strait. Now he was in the archipelago to close the last links in the Northwest Passage.

On April 21, in Pelly Bay, he met an Eskimo named Innookpoozheejook, who was wearing around his head a gold cap band. This Eskimo had never seen white men before; his cap band, so he said, came from a place far away to the west, beyond two rivers, where thirty-five or forty Kabloonas had starved to death. He himself had never been to the spot; did not know where it was; and would not try to point it out on Rae's chart. He could not possibly go so far or even think of accompanying anyone there.

The information was so vague that Rae dared not act on it. Even if he could get to the right locality, what chance would he have, with a foot and a half of snow on the ground, of finding the bodies? When further questioning brought out nothing more, Rae gave up his first impulse to try to find the place Innookpoozheejook described. He bought the gold cap band and told Innookpoozheejook that if any of his friends had other things like it, they should bring them to Repulse Bay; when Rae returned, he would buy them at a good price. With this, Rae and his party headed westward across Boothia.

Six days later, on April 28, they were at the mouth of the tiny Castor and Pollux River, where Dease and Simpson had built their cairn. From here Rae worked northward along the Boothian coast. He satisfied himself that a strait lay between Boothia and King William Land, and on May 6, at Cape Porter, he linked his discoveries with those of Ross. He had had bad weather and the going had been slow; to continue up to the Magnetic Pole and on to Bellot Strait was a greater risk than he was willing to subject his party to. He decided to go no further.

At 1:00 A.M. on May 17 he was back at Pelly Bay, where again he saw the traces of Eskimos and sent two men out to look for them. Eight hours later the men were back with ten or twelve natives—men, women and children. From these people Rae bought a silver spoon and a fork. On the spoon, not engraved, but scratched with a sharp instrument, were the initials F.R.M.C. (Francis Rawdon Moira Crozier, the leader of the retreating crews). The initials puzzled Rae. He was not only unfamiliar with the Christian names of Franklin's officers, but he was strongly of the opinion that the *Erebus* and *Terror* had been lost far west of King William

177

Land. To the best of his knowledge, Captain McClure, however, had been in the north, unheard from, since 1850. Perhaps
the initials were those of McClure, with the small "c" between
the "M.C." left out. Rae took the spoon and paid for it, and
went on his way.

Six days later, back at Repulse Bay, Rae found many Pelly
Bay Eskimos waiting for him with white men's things that
had come from the same place as the gold cap band. Like
Innookpoozheejook, none of the Eskimos at Pelly Bay had
been to the place where the Kabloonas' bodies were. All that
they knew about it was hearsay, but there was no mistaking
the objects that they had. There was Franklin's Guelphic
Order of Hanover, and a small silver plate with his name engraved on it. There were twenty-three silver forks and
spoons, almost all of them marked with the initials or crests
of officers aboard the *Erebus* and the *Terror*. There were
three parts of gold watch cases. Among numerous other things
were a surgeon's scalpel and knife, two pieces of gold watch
chain, a pocket chronometer case, a pocket compass box and
a piece of flannel undervest marked "F.D.V. 1845" (Frederick
Des Voeux, Mate in the *Erebus*).

All the Eskimos had the same story to tell. Four years before
(actually it was six), some forty white men had been seen on
the coast of King William Land, traveling south across the
ice and dragging a boat. They could not speak the native
tongue, but they made it clear by signs that they had left their
ships in the ice to the north and were on their way to the
continent to hunt caribou. Later the Eskimos found the bodies
of some thirty men and a boat and a tent on the mainland, and
five more bodies on an island not far away, both places a long
day's journey to the northwest of a large river. Rae, from the

Eskimos' description, had no difficulty in identifying the river as the Great Fish River. He further concluded that the five bodies were on Montreal Island, the others on the coast of Adelaide Peninsula. At the boat place, the Eskimos said, much powder out of kegs had been dumped in a heap on the ground, and on the island they found the body of an officer with his telescope strapped over his shoulders and his double-barreled gun underneath him. "From the mutilated state of many of the bodies and the contents of the kettles"—so wrote Rae later—"it is evident that our wretched Countrymen had been driven to the last dread alternative, as a means of prolonging life."

All unwitting, Rae had stumbled on the solution of the Franklin mystery. The *Erebus* and the *Terror* had been abandoned in the ice, and some of their officers and men had died on the continent south of King William Island. Rae immediately offered large rewards for any information about survivors, even possible survivors, but got none. The natives were certain that no white man still lived; all of them had been dead for four years. Rae had now to decide whether he would make, so late in the season, a risky attempt to get to the place where the men of the Franklin expedition had died, or return as quickly as possible to England with his news. The thaw was at hand, he had no light boat or canoe to cross the Great Fish River. Should he return late from the journey, he might be unable to supply himself and his party for another winter in the North. With the Franklin men dead, it was better to get his news into the hands of the Admiralty, which could then recall to safety any expeditions still searching in the wrong quarters. He left Repulse Bay August 4, and on the last day of the month was back at York Factory. There, on September

21, 1854, he boarded the *Prince of Wales* for England, where he arrived on October 22.

To Jane, Rae's news was a new life. Only a few months before it had seemed that little more would ever be learned about the fate of her husband. Now, after years of waiting and groping, she had the relief of certainty. With the Crimean War on, the Admiralty could not spare ships or officers to follow up Rae's clues. It turned to the Hudson's Bay Company, with the request that in the following year the company send an expedition down the Great Fish River to verify Rae's report. At the head of the expedition the company put Chief Factor James Anderson of Fort Simpson, then in charge of the Mackenzie River district, and on July 30, 1855 Anderson and his men, in two birch bark canoes, were at the rapids below the outlet of Franklin Lake.

They had been eighteen days coming down the Great Fish River—eighteen days of unspeakable weather, with continuous rain, hail and snow—worse, if possible, than the weather Back had experienced. If Rae's information was correct, they were now on the verge of Franklin discoveries; they had only to get to Montreal Island and to the adjacent coast of Adelaide Peninsula. At the rapids they fell in with natives who had tent poles and kayak paddles made from oars, several pieces of boards, copper and tin kettles and tureens, even a brass letter-nip with the date 1843 on it. Anderson had no interpreter, but the natives made it clear "by pressing the abdomen inwards, pointing to the mouth, and shaking their heads piteously, that these things came from a kayak, the people belonging to which had died of starvation." When shown books and papers, they denied having ever seen anything like them before.

Two days later Anderson was at Montreal Island. On a high ridge of rocks at the southeast corner he and his men came across several metal objects—chisels and a blacksmith's shovel and a chain-hook, also a piece of snowshoe with MR. STANLEY (Surgeon in the *Erebus*) cut in it. A little down from the ridge were a large number of chips and shavings and end planks, as if a boat or part of a boat had been cut up by the natives. In another spot the quick eyes of one searcher fell on a piece of the leather lining of a backgammon board— the same board Jane had put on the *Erebus*. Nowhere did they find a single human remain.

Ice held the party on Montreal Island until August 5, when, in fine weather, they crossed to the mainland. They examined the coast from Elliot Bay to Point Pechell, but found nothing. By then ice had so damaged their canoes that they were rickety and unsafe. Ahead, the pack was firmly grounded; it did not float even at high tide. The way by water was blocked. Two men stayed behind to mend and gum the canoes, while the rest of the party struck out for Point Ogle on foot. They were a day getting there, and saw not a sign of a body or a relic on the way. They found Point Ogle as desolate and bleak as Back had. At this northernmost limit of their journey they picked up, as a treasure trove, a small length of cod line and a two-inch piece of striped cotton; that was all.

The next day, in an inflatable boat, some of the party crossed over to examine Maconochie Island. Anderson wanted to go to Richardson Point, but driving ice stopped him. On August 9, over snow-covered ground, they got back to the canoes. With such frail craft, they dared not linger and a day later they were once more at the mouth of the Great Fish River. They had learned little more than Rae had been told.

If there had once been bodies on Montreal Island or the near-by coast of Adelaide Peninsula, they were no longer there.

In January, 1856, the Admiralty received Anderson's report and washed its hands of any further searching. Three months later they awarded Rae ten thousand pounds for having ascertained the fate of the Franklin expedition. At the time when the Admiralty received its official report from Anderson, Lady Franklin had a letter from him. He told her of his journey and, in detail, of the relics he had found. He was sorry not to have accomplished more, but felt he had turned up everything that would be found on the ground he had covered. The next try, he thought, should be made from the north. A ship should go as close as possible to King William Island, and sledge parties from the ship should follow the trail of the Franklin men as they retreated.

In March the Crimean War ended; with peace, Jane thought, perhaps the Admiralty could be persuaded at least to help another search expedition. In June many eminent persons petitioned the Prime Minister for a final expedition; in July the reply came that it was too late in the year to send one. Jane thought again of using the *Isabel*, this time under the American explorer Kane, but the plan fell through. In April, 1857, the Admiralty refused her the use of its one-time arctic search ship, the *Resolute*. Jane knew then that she would have to make the final effort to solve the mystery of the Franklin expedition herself.

There was no doubt in Jane's mind what to do. She bought the screw schooner yacht *Fox*, of 177 tons burden, and asked Leopold McClintock to take command. He accepted, and immediately work began refitting the ship. There was no time to waste; at the latest the expedition would have to be under way by July. Jane bore £7,000 of the expenses; friends and sympathizers helped with another £3,000. The Admiralty was suddenly generous with stores and clothing and equipment of every kind. Workmen stripped the yacht of her velvet hangings and fine furniture and turned her into an arctic search ship. Outside, they sheathed the whole vessel with planking; inside, they strengthened her with cross beams. They spared nothing to protect her from the ice; she would be alone in the North, with no other ship to fall back on. She was provisioned for twenty-eight months. There were five officers and twenty-one men aboard, with Lieutenant William R. Hobson second in command. Of these twenty-six, seventeen had already taken part in Franklin searches. The course of action was left to McClintock. He knew best how to get to King William Island and how best to conduct the search. Jane's only instructions were contained in a letter: first, to rescue any possible survivors; second, to recover any documents and personal relics of her husband and his party; and third, to determine if possible whether the expedition had been first to discover the Northwest Passage.

Jane and Sophy traveled to Aberdeen, and on the last day of June they visited the ship to say good-by. For Jane, as she came ashore, there was a spontaneous three cheers. McClintock, knowing her distaste for any public demonstration, had tried to stop the salute; it had come out despite his efforts, and Jane was deeply touched. She never liked seeing expeditions off, this one no better than any of the others. But perhaps when McClintock came back she would have the answers to the many questions that had been troubling her for so long.

6.

The *Fox* made a good crossing of the Atlantic and a good run up the west coast of Greenland. On August 19, in Melville Bay, the ship was trapped in the ice and held tight. For two hundred and fifty days—all through the long winter that followed—she drifted southward. On April 25, 1858, in Davis Strait, 1,385 miles from Melville Bay, she was free again. She then put in at Holsteinsborg on the Greenland coast just above the Arctic Circle, and on May 8, for a second time, she headed north for Lancaster Sound. She sailed through the sound and stopped at Beechey Island, and from there, on the morning of August 16, she headed westward through ice-free waters toward Peel Sound, which she reached the evening of the next day.

McClintock did not have the luck in Peel Sound that the *Erebus* and the *Terror* had had. Twenty-five miles south of the entrance he ran into a barrier of solid ice stretching from shore to shore; the way to King William Island was blocked. McClintock turned back into Barrow Strait and headed for Prince Regent Inlet. It was still early in the season; perhaps he could get through Bellot Strait. On August 21 he reached Brentford Bay and the eastern entrance to the strait; the next day he pushed the *Fox* halfway through, and was then stopped by heavy pack.

On September 6 he made another attempt to force his way through, and this time he was successful. But two miles beyond the western end of the strait he was stopped again by heavy floes, fixed in place by hundreds of islets and rocks. McClintock waited a few days to see if winds and tides might loosen the floes, but they remained fast. On September 11 he returned to Brentford Bay. A few days later the *Fox* went into winter quarters at Port Kennedy, near a creek that flowed into a narrow arm of the sea at the foot of a sugar-loaf hill.

Early winter passed with the party occupied by plans and preparations for the coming sledge journeys. On February 17, with Petersen as interpreter, one other man, and two dog sledges and fifteen dogs, McClintock set out for the Magnetic Pole, where he hoped to meet natives who would know something about the Franklin expedition. By March 1 the party was at the Magnetic Pole; they had traced the last major unexplored stretch of the continental coast, but had seen no natives.

Despite short rations and the death of six of his fifteen dogs, McClintock thought that one more day of travel could be squeezed out—one more day to try to pick up the trail of Eskimos. The day proved disappointing. At its end, when the party was about to make camp, McClintock turned around and saw four Eskimos following him. They had been sealing, they told Petersen, and were on their way back to their village. On the dress of one of these natives was a naval button. It came, they said, from where white men had starved on an island near a river. The iron that their knives were made of came from the same place. The two parties traveled on together for an hour until sunset, when the natives built a snow house in which everyone settled for the night.

The next morning they continued together, presumably toward the Eskimo village. When ten miles of traveling had not brought the village within sight, McClintock decided to go no farther. He would gladly barter for any white men's belongings the Eskimos' friends had, but the friends must bring such belongings to him. The natives quickly put up a snow house, and McClintock displayed his articles of barter —knives, files, needles, scissors, beads, and other trinkets. The natives departed, and the next morning were back with their fellow villagers, forty-five in all. Almost all had something from the missing expedition. They had silver spoons and forks, a medal that once belonged to Mr. A. Macdonald (Assistant-Surgeon in the *Terror*), a part of a gold chain, several buttons, and many articles—knives and bows and arrows—made of iron and wood that once had been parts of a boat. Like Rae's informants, none of these natives had seen the white men alive; one, but only one, had seen their bones on the island where they died.

Petersen, struggling with the natives' dialect, questioned the Eskimos as closely as he could for precise details. The story he got was that a ship had been crushed in the ice to the west of King William Island. Everybody aboard had landed safe; later the ship sank—before the Eskimos got anything off her. An old man, Oonalee, said that it was an eight days' journey to where the ship had gone down, and when asked in what direction, he pointed with his spear to Cape Felix. The sum total of the information was scanty; it added nothing to what Rae had learned five years before. The natives promised that they would still be on the west coast of Boothia in the spring, when McClintock would be traveling south on his way to King William Island. Perhaps they would have more to tell him then. With this, McClintock left to go back to the *Fox*.

In order to cover as wide an area as possible, the plan for the spring search fell into three parts: McClintock was to go down the east side of King William Island to Montreal Island, then return to the ship by the south and west coast of King William Island; Hobson was to cross over to Victoria Land and to search along the shore of what is now McClintock Strait; and Young was to visit the unexplored parts of the coasts of Prince of Wales Island. The search would be primarily for the ships; even if, as the Eskimos said, one ship had sunk, records and other valuable information about the expedition and its members might still be aboard the remaining ship.

On April 2 the two southern search parties were off from Port Kennedy; a few days later the western party struck out for Prince of Wales Island. McClintock and Hobson planned to go together down the Boothian coast as far as Cape Victoria, then separate. In size and equipment their parties were almost identical; each had a sledge drawn by four men and a dog sledge with a driver. The loads worked out at 200 pounds per man and 100 pounds per dog. The interpreter, Petersen, was dog-driver in McClintock's party; and McClintock himself drove five puppies, harnessed for the first time to a small sledge loaded with their own provisions. The puppies they hoped eventually to sell to the Eskimos. The procession moved away from the ship in elegant style, each sledge flying its own gay silk banner—McClintock's a red one margined with white embroidery and bearing in white letters the name of Lady Franklin. Two days after the start, the parties reached the sea. With their tents hoisted on the sledges as sails, the tent poles serving as yards and masts, they headed southward for the Magnetic Pole.

On April 20, at latitude 70° 30′ north, they met two families of Eskimos—twelve in all, among them some of the Eskimos McClintock had met the February before. Petersen again pressed them with questions, and was rewarded for his pains; the natives of King William Island, the Eskimos now said, had seen not one ship, but two. One, as they had said before, had sunk in deep water. The other had been forced ashore by ice, and from her the natives had got a great deal of wood and many other things. They supposed she still remained where the natives had found her; she would probably be much broken; Ootloolik (Ookjoolik) was the name of the place where she grounded. This place, Petersen and McClintock mistakenly made out, was somewhere on the west coast of King William Island. The body of a big man with long teeth had been found aboard the ship. All the white men had gone away to the "large river," taking a boat or boats with them. It was August or September when the ships were destroyed, and in the following winter the bones of the white men were found.

Here were the very details McClintock wanted. Both ships were now accounted for: one had sunk and the other could be found on the west coast of King William Island. He had the information too late to spare Young a fruitless search on Prince of Wales Island, but there was still time to change Hobson's plans. In the face of the almost positive clue to the whereabouts of the remaining Franklin ship, McClintock stuck to his plan to go himself down the east side of King William Island, and sent Hobson to explore the west coast. If anything from the lost expedition was there, young Hobson would have the honor of discovery. A few days later the two parties reached Cape Victoria and there separated, McClintock to cross to Port Parry, Hobson to Cape Felix.

On May 4, off the southwest tip of Matty Island, McClintock came across some abandoned snow houses, in all of which were shavings and chips of wood from the ships and gear of the missing expedition. From then on, it was to be like this—in almost every snow house McClintock entered, he found some ghostly evidence of the Franklin expedition. Fog kept the party near Matty Island for two days; on the third day, to avoid snow blindness, they began traveling at night. About halfway down the east coast of King William Island, near Cape Norton, they came to an occupied village of ten or twelve snow houses. Here McClintock, at four needles each, bought six pieces of silver plate, all of it marked with the crests or initials of Franklin, Crozier, Fairholme or Macdonald. He also bought bows and arrows of English wood, and was offered a sledge obviously made of wood from a ship. The natives told him it was five days' journey to the wrecked Franklin ship—one day up an inlet and four days overland. There had been books on the ship, they said, but all of them the weather had destroyed. As for the white men, many of them had dropped by the way as they went to the Great River; some were buried and some were not. The natives to whom he was talking had themselves found a few of the bodies, but they had seen none of the Kabloonas alive. The wreck, they believed, had not shifted from where the natives had found it first; only a year ago an old woman and a boy had visited it.

McClintock continued down the coast. Off Point Booth,

on May 10, he found a single snow house with a number of wooden articles outside it, among them two snow shovels made of thin plank, painted pale yellow or white, apparently the bottom boards of a boat. The occupants of the house, a terrified old man and woman, were less than helpful. They protested that the wood they had came from other natives; they knew of the Great Fish River, but it was a long way off; and they had heard nothing of white men dying on King William Island. Their fear of the white men was such that there was plainly nothing to be gained in pressing them further, and McClintock went on his way. Quite unaware, he was now almost in the tracks of the retreating Franklin crews. He passed Keeuna, cut across Point Ogle, and camped on the ice of the estuary of the Great Fish River. On May 15 he was on Montreal Island. There, near a native marker, Petersen picked up several small pieces of tin and iron, probably part of the loot from the boat; no one else found anything. The party crossed the ice to the east coast of Adelaide Peninsula, examined the coast south to Elliot Bay, and then began the return journey. So far their luck had been fair; they had found a trail marked by relics and they had got new information from the Eskimos. But of the ship itself or of any records or of human remains, they had not found a trace.

McClintock headed overland to Barrow Inlet and spent a day examining it. He had hoped to meet natives there, but encountered none. He cut across the base of Point Richardson; he was then almost on the spot where the last Franklin survivors had died, but deep snow covered the low ground, and he saw nothing to rouse his suspicions. He turned north and followed up the western shore of Point Richardson and across Simpson Strait to King William Island, striking it west of the Peffer River. Two of the graves he sought were east of the river.

Once more the party was on the actual path of the retreating crews; they made for Cape Herschel, traveling on the ice close to shore. The snow-covered beach offered little hope of spotting any remains; on the other hand, markers or cairns would stand out sharply against the white. They passed Douglas Bay and Tulloch Point and saw nothing. A little west of Gladman Point they came to a cairn nearly five feet high; it had an old look about it, as if it had been built long before the Franklin expedition, but McClintock dared take nothing for granted. His men carefully pulled down the cairn, stone by stone, and broke the earth beneath with a pickax; no cylinder or container was there.

Just after midnight on the twenty-fifth of May luck favored them. McClintock was walking slowly along a gravel ridge above the beach. The ridge was bare of snow in spots, and for this reason offered some encouragement to the searchers. On coming to a place where the snow was shallow McClintock looked down and saw the back of a bleached human skull; near it were some bits of clothing that stuck up through the snow, and not far away a rock. Removal of the snow disclosed the skeleton of a young man. It lay face down, as if the man had been sitting on the rock and had fallen forward and died. To judge from the clothing, the man had been a steward or an officer's servant. Close by lay a clothes brush and a comb with a few light brown hairs still in it. There was no doubt that the man had come from the *Erebus* or the *Terror*; at least one of the expedition's members had completed the Northwest Passage. The proof no longer hung on the accuracy of Eskimo stories; the man's skeleton told the tale beyond dispute. But who was he? What was his name? The clue lay in a pocketbook found nearby. It and all its contents were frozen hard and could not safely be examined at the time. When thawed, the pocketbook was found to contain among other things a parchment seaman's certificate, on which the writing had faded so badly as to be unreadable. In England, chemicals applied to restore the writing brought out the name and description of Harry Peglar, Captain of the Foretop of the *Terror*.

A day later McClintock and his party were at Cape Herschel. Here at Simpson's cairn the survivors must surely have left a record. The appearance of the cairn was not encouraging—obviously, it had been tampered with. No longer "lofty," as Simpson described it, it was scarcely four feet high, with the south side pulled down and the central stones removed; the hollow space was filled with snow. A search revealed no record; if once the cairn had contained a message from the retreating parties, the natives had found it and carried it away. There was still hope that something might be buried underneath. The men struggled to pull up three large limestone slabs that had been laid one on top of another. They then broke up the frozen ground with a pickax, but their efforts were unrewarded.

Twelve miles from Cape Herschel, across Washington Bay, McClintock found a small cairn that marked Hobson's extreme. Hobson had been there six days before and had left a note containing a brief report of his discoveries.

He had parted from McClintock on the twenty-eighth of April at Cape Victoria and headed for Cape Felix, which he reached at two o'clock on the afternoon of May 2. There he left a depot of provisions for nine days, and on the morning of the third started down the west coast. At 9:15, three miles beyond Cape Felix, he came upon a large cairn, and near it three tents—the summer camp of the Franklin men. Many of the stones had fallen off the top of the cairn; among the stones lay two broken bottles. These had doubtless once contained records, but without the bottles to protect the records, the papers had long ago rotted or blown away. In the cairn Hobson uncovered a piece of blank paper folded in a triangular shape. Whatever message had once been on it was faded beyond recovery; not even a dot, not the faintest line remained.

The three tents lay flat in the snow, some nine feet from the cairn. Inside the tents were blankets and bearskins and warm clothing; there were also packages of needles, pipes, the eyepiece of a small telescope, and three blue beads. Outside, recovered by Hobson's men from beneath the snow, were some broken cups of blue and white china, the device from the front of a marine's shako, a potato tin, a small copper stove, a bag of gunpowder, and a canister with the word "cheese" scratched on it. Hobson's party uncovered three fireplaces, and near them some matches, ptarmigan feathers, salt meat bones, and the jaw of a fox. Hobson concluded that a party of ten or twelve men had camped at the spot for some time and had left, probably for the ships, in a hurry. How else explain why they left so much behind? All the day of Hobson's arrival at the cairn, until six in the evening, he and his men searched the place, and again for five hours the next morning. Satisfied that they had missed little, they proceeded down the coast.

At the end of an hour's march they came to a small cairn; it was empty. The next day they found a telltale piece of driftwood—a length of white spruce that had been cut with the grain with a whip saw. It was Hobson's opinion that it had been sawed on the spot and the other piece used for fuel. The sawing was unquestionably the work of white men. On the morning of the sixth, at Ross's Victory Point, they saw a cairn and beside it an empty tin canister and a pickax with a broken helve. An hour's search turned up nothing more. Hobson took the pickax and left the canister, and he and his party continued south along the low, curving shore. They had still not seen a sign of the wreck the Eskimos had described; it was probably farther down the coast.

At 11:15 the same morning, three and a half miles beyond Ross's Victory Point, they came to a big cairn; near it was a great strew of clothing, personal articles, and miscellaneous gear. Everything lay just as the Franklin men had left it when they lightened their load at their first landing place. Nothing had been touched; apparently not a soul had been at the place since Crozier and the one hundred and four men under his command had landed there after abandoning their ships. In among some loose stones that had fallen off the top of the cairn, Hobson picked up a metal cylinder. The top was on, but not soldered; when Hobson pulled the cap off, he found the rolled-up tide paper inside. It was spotted with rust and one corner had rotted away, but the writing was clear and legible.

At the top was the message left by Gore in May, 1847, in the ruins of the cairn built by Ross at Victory Point. It gave the date and the position of the ships off Cape Felix. Then it said:

Having wintered in 1846-7 at Beechey Island in Lat 74°. 43'.28″ N. Long 91°.39'.15″ W. After having ascended Well-

ington Channel to Lat. 77°, and returned by the West side of
Cornwallis Island.
Sir John Franklin commanding the Expedition.
All well.
Party consisting of 2 officers and 6 men left the Ships on
Monday 24th May, 1847.
Gm. Gore, Lieut.
Chas. F. Des Voeux. Mate.

The mistake in the date of the winter at Beechey Island
caught Hobson's eye. He knew that they had wintered at
Beechey in 1845-46; the grave markers at the island had told
that. But dates were hard to keep track of in the North; it
was a natural mistake to make. He turned the paper sideways,
and his eye hurried on to what was written around the margins.

[25th April, 1]848. H. M. Ship[s] Terror and Erebus were
deserted on the 22nd April, 5 leagues NNW of this [hav]ing
been beset since 12 Septr. 1846. The Officers & Crews consisting of 105 souls—under the command [of Cap]tain FRM
Crozier landed here—in Lat 69°.37'.42" Long 98° 41' [This
p]aper was found by Lt Irving under the cairn supposed to
have been built by Sir James Ross in 1831 4 miles to the Northward—where it had been deposited by the late Commander
Gore in June 1847. Sir James Ross' pillar has not however been
found and the paper has been transferred to this position which
is that in which Sir J Ross' pillar was erected—Sir John Franklin died on the 11th June 1847 and the total loss by deaths in
the Expedition has been to this date 9 officers & 15 men

FRM Crozier   James Fitzjames Captain
Captain & Senior Offr   HMS Erebus

and start on to-morrow 26th
for Backs Fish River

Everywhere lay relics of the expedition. Near the cairn was the four-foot pile of clothing, not a piece of it marked, and all the pockets empty. There were pickaxes and shovels and iron hoops and boats' cooking stoves. There was a piece of copper lightning conductor; there were some brass curtain rods. Why had they brought these from the ships in the first place? Where did they expect to meet thunderstorms or hang curtains? Many of the things bore their owners' names: the top of Mr. Osmer's mahogany gun case, Private Wilkes's clothes brush, Mr. Hornsby's sextant and W. Mark's pannikin. There was part of a tent, an oar sawed in half with a blanket nailed to its flat side, and a ship's medicine chest. The things lay strewn about, a record of desperate haste and desperate measures. All that day Hobson and his men searched, to make certain they had missed nothing. With the morning of May 7 he copied the record they had found and put the copy in the cairn; the original he kept on his person. Shortly after eleven o'clock the party resumed its march southward. If the ships had been abandoned where the record said, in all probability one of them would be found to the south, brought up on the western shoulder of land.

From the 9th to the 16th a continuous northwest gale made traveling arduous and kept the party tent-bound for two whole days and parts of three others. Often, the heavy snow made it impossible to see anything at all. Thinking they were on the sea, they one time followed a frozen water course and camped on a lake four miles inland. They passed Erebus Bay and Terror Bay and rounded the western shoulder of the island; still they saw nothing. In this weather they could well have passed the wreck of a ship without seeing it; Hobson did not know whether he had missed a Franklin ship or not. The bad weather continued. Hobson came down with scurvy but struggled on to the spot near Cape Herschel where he built the cairn and left the message for McClintock.

With this information, McClintock went on his way along the southern coast to Cape Crozier, which he rounded on the 29th of May. At Erebus Bay he came upon a boat which Hobson, according to a note, had found a few days before. It was the boat that the party from Terror Bay had taken thus far on their return journey to the ships. Headed up the coast for the next point of land to the northeast, she was still on her sledge, though partially out of the cradle and heeling somewhat to starboard. "She was built," as McClintock wrote, "with a view to lightness and light draught of water, and evidently equipped with the utmost care for the ascent of the Great Fish River; she had neither oars nor rudder, paddles supplying their place; and as a large remnant of light canvas, commonly known as No. 8, was found, and also a small block for reeving a sheet through, I suppose she had been provided with a sail. A sloping canvas roof or rain-awning had also formed part of her equipment. She was fitted with a weathercloth 9 inches high, battened down all round the gunwale, and supported by 24 iron stanchions, so placed as to serve likewise for rowing thowells. There was a deep-sea sounding line, fifty fathoms long, near her, as well as an ice-grapnel; this line must have been intended for river work as a track line." To all appearances, she lay right where she had been left eleven years before.

There was much clothing in her, a few books, towels, saws, files, shot, knives, scabbards, etc. There was an empty pemmican tin marked with the letter "E"; the only food was some tea and forty pounds of chocolate. In her also were two skeletons—one, in the bow, of a young man; the other, in the stern, of a middle-aged man of good size. Near the skeleton in the stern stood two guns, one against each side of the boat. Each had one barrel discharged and the other loaded. Close to the skeleton in the stern were five watches, fifteen silver spoons, and eleven silver forks, eight pieces of which bore Franklin's crest. These two men must have been the last survivors of the camp at Erebus Bay. They had taken up residence in the boat to await the return of their comrades from the ship. The man in the bow had died first. The man in the stern had gathered the treasure about him, doubly armed himself with his own and his companion's gun, and carried out to the end his last and lonely vigil in the North.

McClintock turned from the spot, deep in grief. The sight had made too poignant the sufferings of those who had to abandon the *Erebus* and the *Terror*. He and his party now continued to Crozier's landing place, which they reached on June 2. There a note from Hobson said that he had found, south of Back Bay, a cylinder with a second note in it left by Gore. It was a duplicate of the one left at Ross's Victory Point, with nothing added. On June 19 McClintock was back at the *Fox;* in seventy-nine days he had made a journey of nearly 1,200 miles. Hobson had reached the ship five days before, so ill with scurvy that he could neither walk nor stand without help. On the 27th Young returned from his futile search on Prince of Wales Island.

McClintock had done well the job he set out to do. He had not found the wrecks of the ships, to be sure, but he had solved the mystery of where the ships had been abandoned and where the crews had gone. He had recovered neither log-books nor journals, but he was persuaded from the condition in which the Franklin men had traveled and from the tales of the Eskimos that the papers of the expedition were gone forever. And he was taking back to Lady Franklin one thing of great importance to her—positive proof that her husband's expedition had completed the Northwest Passage, the first men known to have done so.

By the 16th of July the *Fox* was almost ready for sea. On the 9th of August a south wind moved the ice out of Port Kennedy, and the *Fox* was free. On September 20, 1859, she was in the English Channel, home after twenty-seven months. It was fourteen years and four months and one day since the *Erebus* and the *Terror* had sailed. Thus long the outside world had waited for firsthand news of the expedition's fate; now that news had come. Jane's refusal to give up the search had been justified. To her the *Fox* brought back a small but special comfort: of all the wives left behind, she alone knew with certainty the date of her husband's death.

7.

In McClintock's opinion further searching was useless. He had accounted for both ships; he believed that all the
journals and logbooks had long ago rotted away or been destroyed by the natives; he was certain that no survivors still
lived. One hundred and five men had abandoned the *Erebus*
and the *Terror* and had started for Back's Fish River and died
on the way. Eskimos had found some of their bodies on the
continent and some on an island near by. Why should any
more lives be risked in searching, when there was so little hope
of finding anything of importance?

In America a dissenting voice was raised. There, in Cincinnati, Charles Francis Hall, an arctic enthusiast of quite a
different caliber from McClintock, called for still another
effort. Hall, born in Rochester, New Hampshire, had begun
his working life as a blacksmith in the town of his birth. Later
he moved west to Cincinnati, where he opened a stationery
store, worked as a seal engraver, and for a brief time owned
and published two newspapers—first *The Occasional* and
then *The Penny Press*. He dabbled in scientific invention and
at one time was so enthusiastic about a caloric engine that his

Cincinnati neighbors, in a play on his initials, dubbed him "Caloric Fool" Hall.

The Arctic fascinated Hall; its explorers were his heroes, and he himself had often dreamed of discovering the Pole. He had followed the Franklin search in its smallest details, reading every available book. In talks with whalers from the North he learned that white men living an Eskimo life among Eskimos stayed healthy and well. Might not, then, some of Franklin's men still survive? The more Hall pondered, the more the possibility became a certainty. After fourteen years of doubt, he was suddenly sure that the fate of at least some of Franklin's men had been revealed to him; also that he had been commanded by a higher power to rescue the survivors from the heathen. Specifically, he should go to King William Island, live among the Eskimos, listen to their stories, and find out where the white men were. He would then do his Christian duty of returning them to civilization. Once Hall had received and interpreted his message, nothing could turn him from obeying it. Early in 1860, at the age of thirty-nine, he left his wife and two children and set out for the North.

In May, from New London, Connecticut, he sailed on a whaler to Cumberland Sound, on the southeast coast of Baffin Land. With him, as almost sole equipment, he had a 28-foot boat in which he planned to go up Cumberland Sound to its western end; cross by stream and lake and portage to Foxe Basin, north of Hudson Bay; then, by way of Fury and Hecla Strait, go on to Boothia and the Franklin country. He intended to take no white companions but to make the whole journey with native help. Shortly after his arrival at Cumberland Sound a gale dashed his boat to pieces and with it his first plan for reaching King William Island.

For two years he stayed on at Cumberland Sound, accustoming himself to native life and becoming firm friends with a remarkable Eskimo couple, Joe and Hannah by name. Twenty-five years before, the couple had caught the fancy of a Hull merchant, Mr. Bolby, who had taken them with him from Baffin Land to England. There they were married and much sought after. They dined with Queen Victoria and the Prince Consort and traveled widely. After two years they returned by choice to their homeland. Both had learned English, Hannah much more fluently than Joe. To Hall, planning a new attempt to get to King William Island, Joe and Hannah looked like an answer to prayer. If they would go with him, he would have a hunter, a housekeeper, and two interpreters. In the interval before he could set his new plans in motion he busied himself mapping Frobisher Bay and gathering Eskimo tales about Frobisher himself. The natives' stories, three hundred years after the events they chronicled, were amazingly accurate. They confirmed Hall's belief that from the Eskimos on King William Island he could get true and detailed accounts of what had happened to the Franklin expedition and its survivors. His friendship for Joe and Hannah deepened into affection; they in turn came to a touching respect for his honesty, his fearlessness, and his kindness. They agreed to accompany Hall to the United States and then, as soon as sufficient funds could be raised, set out with him for King William Island by way of Repulse Bay. In August, 1862, Hall left Cumberland Sound for New London and New York, to seek support for his new Franklin search; with him went Joe and Hannah and their little child Tukerlita—Butterfly.

The task Hall set himself would have dismayed a less courageous and dedicated man. While raising funds for his new expedition to the North, he had also to support both himself and his Eskimos—and all this in the midst of the Civil War, with the national mind and purse concentrated on that struggle. For two years he labored incessantly; he worked on a book that he hoped would bring in funds; he lectured, with Joe and Hannah on stage in full native dress; he turned everywhere he could for help. The return from the lectures was disappointingly small, not enough even to pay for the Eskimos' support. Added to this disappointment was bereavement; on the last day of February, 1863, Tukerlita died at the age of eighteen months. Henry Grinnell, a New York merchant who had already generously contributed to many Franklin searches, offered Hall his friendship and backing, but the United States Senate, the New York State Legislature, and the New York Chamber of Commerce turned down all Hall's appeals for funds. The Navy Department refused to lend him instruments. Still Hall persisted. "What burned within my soul like a living fire all the time," he later wrote, "was the full faith that I should find some survivors of Sir John's memorable Expedition living among the natives, and that I would be the instrument in the hand of heaven, of their salvation." Hall cut his plans—and the help he was asking for—to the bone. He asked that a whaler take him and Joe and Hannah to Wager Bay. From there they would get to Repulse Bay in their own boat, then go on to King William by sledge. But at the end of almost two years of effort and pleading, it looked as if support for even so modest an expedition could not be obtained.

On May 4, 1864, Hall lectured before the Long Island Historical Society. A few days later an appeal for funds to support Hall, the appeal signed by influential backers, appeared in the leading New York newspapers. The press endorsed the appeal; subscriptions began to flow in; Hall's minimum expenses were guaranteed.

On June 30 of the same year the whaler *Monticello*, under Captain E. A. Chapel, of Hudson, New York, sailed from New London for Depot Island, off the western shore of Hudson Bay between Chesterfield Inlet and the southern entrance to Roes Welcome. Aboard were Hall and Joe and Hannah, equipment and supplies for the expedition, and the essential whaleboat—the *Sylvia*, named after Mr. Grinnell's daughter. Two United States gunboats, the *Iasco* and the *Marblehead*, stood by at the *Monticello's* departure, their rigging manned and their flags dipped. Hall was brimming with hope; at last he was on his way, much after the fashion he had once confided to his journal. "God only knows my struggles," he had written. "But, single-handed and alone, I will yet accomplish my purpose—for I know it is a just and noble one—or die in attempting it."

A month later, after a stop at St. John's, Newfoundland, the *Monticello* was at Depot Island. Here Hall engaged Charles Rudolph, from the whaler *Isabel*, to accompany him on his journey. Rudolph had once spent a winter among the Eskimos, and he came to Hall highly recommended. On August 29 the *Monticello's* tender carried Hall and his party up Roes Welcome, heading for Wager Bay. The captain mistook his bearings, and on August 31, despite Hall's insistence that a mistake was being made, put the little expedition ashore forty miles south of its destination. Three days later, in the *Sylvia*, the party started northward up the coast of Roes Welcome.

Hall had not gone many miles when, at a place called Noowook, he fell in with hospitable Eskimos from Repulse Bay.

These Eskimos had often encountered American whalers, and had in their possession boats and guns and other articles of civilization. It was too late in the season, they said, to risk crossing the mouth of Wager Bay with a boat so heavily loaded as Hall's. They themselves would be going to Repulse Bay in the spring; Hall could go with them then. If he stayed the winter at Noowook, they would supply him and his companions with walrus, seal, bear, and musk ox meat. Hall and his party settled in.

Soon Hall was pursuing his favorite subject—the Franklin survivors. The natives had heard about the two ships that were abandoned in the ice and about the Kabloonas who had starved or frozen to death. But this was not all. Three of these Noowook natives were brothers, and they had a cousin, Tooshooarthariu, who knew a great deal about Kabloonas. This cousin was far away at the moment, but the brothers would be glad to tell his story.

One day, when Tooshooarthariu, with his family, was out sealing on the ice near Boothia, he met four white men, one of them Crozier. Three of the men were fat, but Crozier looked starved nearly to death; his eyes were so sunken and his face so skeletonlike that Tooshooarthariu could hardly bear to look at him. These four white men were the last survivors of a party that had abandoned their ships in the ice; all the others were dead. The three fat ones had been living on their companions' flesh; Crozier had refused to eat it, that was why he was thin. Tooshooarthariu pitied these men and took them in. He nursed Crozier back to health, giving him the first day a little seal meat and each day after that a little more. One man died of sickness, but Crozier and two others lived. In the spring they went to Boothia, and there they shot many ducks and geese. They lived with the Eskimos, and Crozier grew fat and well. After a time, taking with them a boat they could carry, these three left for the south to go to the white man's country. On parting, Crozier offered Too-shooarthariu his gun, but the Eskimo refused it, he was afraid it would kill him. Crozier gave him a long knife instead. Too-shooarthariu never saw the white men again, but he is certain that they are somewhere, and still alive.

At this story Hall's excitement ran high. Was he not hearing as fact just what he thought had happened? Perhaps Crozier was even now in the North and could be found and saved. Hall must without fail get to King William Island and meet Tooshooarthariu, who must be told—and by Hall—that the whole civilized world would forever remember him for taking pity on Crozier and saving his life and the lives of his two friends. And with Tooshooarthariu's help, Crozier and his companions must be found if they were still alive.

The winter at Noowook wore on endlessly. In the autumn there were seal hunts and bear hunts and walrus hunts. Early in December some of the natives went to Depot Island to visit the whaling fleet. With them departed the white man Rudolph; he had had enough of the search. From the middle of January until the middle of February Hall was with the whalers at Depot Island. When good sledging weather came to Noowook, the natives tried Hall's patience to the limit; day after day they had a new reason for lingering where they were; it seemed they would never get started for Repulse Bay. In March Hall abandoned all hope of getting to King William Island that year. Not until the end of April did he reach Wager Bay, where the natives spent a happy month sealing. On June 5 the parties took to their boats for the journey to

Repulse Bay; eight days later they crossed the mouth of the bay and camped on its northern shores. From then on there was delay of every kind; delay for hunting, a delay of a month while Hannah lay ill with pneumonia, delay to visit with the whalers that came up the bay. Early in September Hall reached Gibson Cove at the upper end of Repulse Bay. At the head of the cove, near Fort Hope, where Rae had spent two winters, Hall put up his encampment. On September 16 Hannah gave birth to a son, Little King William. Through the autumn the caribou hunting was good; one hundred and forty-three were brought in. The year ended with bright prospects for a successful search.

On March 31, 1866, the journey westward got under way. "Now for King William's Land!" wrote Hall in his notebook. "Up at 4 A.M. and getting ready for a start." The party included Hall and Joe and Hannah and Little King William and fifteen more native men, women, and children. There were two sledges, each with its team of dogs. Hall quickly abandoned any idea of speed. Hardly twenty-four hours on the way, the party was snowbound for three days. Then Little King William fell ill, necessitating a week's stop. On April 13 another gale held them up; the Eskimos spent the day feasting and playing dominoes. Then they began to worry lest there be no caribou on Kikerktak and threatened to turn back. Hall, exasperated, vowed that if the natives deserted him, he would go on alone. Again Little King William grew worse; again there was delay. It took the party eighteen days to cross Rae Isthmus and reach the shores of Committee Bay—a journey of forty-five miles.

On the sea ice they gathered momentum, one day making seventeen miles. On May 30, at the northern side of Colville

Bay, near Cape Beaufort, they fell in with Eskimos from Pelly Bay, friends of some of the natives in Hall's party. Hearing of Hall's interest in Franklin, old Kokleearngnun, the head man, produced two silver spoons that he said Crozier had given him, one bearing the initials F.R.M.C. There were other relics too—a pair of scissors, a barometer case, and a silver watch case. Kokleearngnun said that as a boy he had been on the ships frozen in the ice and had met the white chief. He knew about the vessel that went down off Ookjoolik and about the white men who walked to the Great Fish River. More exciting still, in Kokleearngnun's party was the mother of Tooshooarthariu. She talked of her son with Hall, and further told him that not long before a man named Innookpoozheejook—the same Eskimo Rae had met in 1854—had found two boats on sledges on the west coast of Kikerktak. More and more it began to look as if Hall, by revelation or more earthly means, had hit upon the truth of the end of the Franklin expedition. If only he could meet Tooshooarthariu and Innookpoozheejook, he would have final proof.

Unfortunately, Kokleearngnun and his party had other stories to tell—stories of starvation and murder and cannibalism to the west. No sane person, they said, would think of going to Kikerktak. The stories fell on ready ears. Terror seized the Eskimos accompanying Hall; they refused to go any farther. No amount of persuasive reasoning could move them, and a saddened Hall made ready to return to the east. He could only resolve to make another try the following year, with four or five armed white men from the whalers in Repulse Bay. On May 5 he started back; on May 13 Little King William died, the second child Joe and Hannah had lost since they cast their lot with Hall; on May 24 the party reached Repulse Bay.

Now Hall's hopes and plans depended on the good will of whalers. If he could get volunteers from the whaling crews, he would be able to reach King William Island in another sledging season. While he waited for the ships to come, he set to work and mapped Repulse Bay. A good chart of these waters, he thought, would win him favor with the captains. At the end of August the vessels began to arrive, but no captain would release any men for Hall's scheme. By the end of September a poor catch had changed the captains' minds. Four ships decided to stay on another year and winter in Repulse Bay. Under these circumstances Hall could have his five volunteers, on condition that they be back from King William Island before the close of the whaling season in 1867. Again the future looked bright to Hall. On November 24 he moved over to Harbour Islands, where the ships were berthed, and there put up his snow house for the winter. He was used to living in the style of the Eskimos now, and did not want to change. But it gave him a feeling of comfort to have the sight and sound of the ships always so close at hand. The year was now 1866.

In February, 1867, the question of dogs for the journey came up. Hall had several of his own, but needed thirteen more to make up the two teams he needed. For these dogs he had already bargained; for some he had even made payments with tobacco and other articles. To his dismay, he learned that the whaling captains had their eyes on these dogs. The spring whaling season was near at hand; every native and every dog would soon be needed for sledding blubber and bone from the open water to the ships. Had not the captains fed the natives all winter long? If so, the captains certainly had a first right to the use of the men and their sledges. The natives admitted the promises they had made to Hall, but dared not go against the orders of the whaling captains. Hall could not win in such a contest. Discouraged, he withdrew. Three hundred miles to the north, at Igloolik, near Fury and Hecla Strait, dogs could be obtained, Hall was sure. The distance was long, but it was nothing in Hall's mind if he could cover it and get back still in time to journey west in the coming spring. He thought he could.

He took, not Joe and Hannah, but another Eskimo, the Eskimo's wife and child, and a boy. On February 8 he was off. The journey was a repetition of Hall's other journeys with natives—delays and side trips and troubles of every kind. He got his dogs, but lost fifty-two days of precious time in the getting. He was back at the ships on March 31. The whaling season had opened; the captains, despite their promises, would not spare a man to go with Hall to King William Island. For a number of days Hall lay sick and disheartened in his snow house. When one of the captains asked him aboard for tea, Hall answered the invitation with a full confession of his discouragement: "Excuse me captain, if I am not there to tea, for really I feel so overwhelmed in grief at my disappointment in not making the sledge journey for which I have so long been preparing, that I am sure I could not contribute one jot to any one's social enjoyment."

In May Hall journeyed to Cape Weynton on Committee Bay to secure the safety of a cache he had made there the year before. The summer passed uneventfully; autumn came. When the whaleships left, five volunteers stayed behind to go with him on his spring search.

That winter, 1868, Hall heard stories of white men seen as recently as three years before on the northwest corner of Melville Peninsula. Might not these be the very survivors he was looking for? In April, with Joe and Hannah and an Eskimo family and one of the volunteers, Hall journeyed north to investigate. He found a white man's cairn, but of the white men themselves he saw nothing at all. It was the end of June before he got back to Repulse Bay; it was then far too late to start for King William Island.

While Hall had been away, the volunteers had grown more and more discontent with their lot. On his return, the discontent showed itself in open ill-feeling and laxness in their work. On July 31 mutiny broke out, and Hall, in self-defense, shot the ringleader. For two weeks the victim lived on, while Hall did everything possible to save his life. He did not succeed. With the man's death, Hall's dark moments reached their blackest. Now, unless a whaler came into Repulse Bay soon, he would have to take the remaining volunteers back to York Factory in his boat. That would mean abandonment, after four years of labor and endless patience, of all his hopes and plans. On August 16 two whaling vessels arrived, and the four volunteers shipped for home. Hall stayed on at Repulse Bay. In another spring he would make his journey westward. He would find Tooshooarthariu and Innookpoozheejook; he would save the Franklin survivors. He would do it with no help but that of Joe and Hannah and a few other natives.

In February and March preparations for the spring journey got under way. Day after day the slow work of drying venison over native lamps went on; in the end 680 pounds fresh had been reduced to 170 dry. This dried venison mixed with toodnoo (caribou fat) made good pemmican. Six hundred lead balls for ammunition were molded over a coal fire in a stove. The arms were got ready—guns, bayonets, spears, knives and pistols.

On March 23 the journey began. The party consisted of Hall and Joe and Hannah and nine other Eskimos—four men, two women and two children. There were eighteen dogs. The two sledges—*Grinnell* and *Brevoort*—weighed, with their loads, a total of 5,245 pounds, making an average pull of 292 pounds for each dog. The runners of the *Brevoort* were sixteen feet long and ten inches deep, and its seventeen crossbars were each just an inch under three feet. The party got off in a gale; the wind was of force eight and snow drift filled the air for a few feet up; above the drift the air was beautifully clear.

Day after day the party moved along at a fair pace. They made Cape Weynton in ten days; in 1866 it had taken twenty-eight. They followed along the track of Hall's first journey—the same route followed by Rae in 1854. On April 11 they reached the shore of Pelly Bay; the next day, far out on the ice, they came to a cluster of snow houses and met the native inhabitants, among them Kobbig, Kokleearngnun's brother. These Eskimos had several Franklin relics: a sword point four inches long; a gallon stone jug, pinkish in color; a snow shovel made of wood from a ship that sank after the natives tore a hole in her side. Kobbig knew about the white men who had come to Kikerktak in two ships. Most of them had died, he said, but two were still alive, one of the two Crozier. He himself had friends who had seen these two. When asked the friends' names, Kobbig replied, "Innookpoozheejook and

Tooshooarthariu." Tooshooarthariu, he said, could be found on Kikerktak. Innookpoozheejook was at the estuary of the Great Fish River; Innookpoozheejook was very ill.

With this news Hall continued on his way. Two weeks later he reached the western side of Boothia and started out on the ice across Shepherd Bay. Off Point Dryden he came upon an empty snow house with fresh tracks leading to the south. Following these, Hall's party came in sight of a village, near which a number of men with dogs were sealing. Fear seized the natives accompanying Hall. He ordered camp made at a safe distance, a mile or so away, and put off the meeting until the following day.

The next morning with a sledge and nine of the best dogs the men of the party set out. Three hundred yards from the village Hall halted them. From there three of his men, armed with sharp knives, went on toward the native encampment. Hall watched anxiously to see what would happen. The Eskimos of the village came out from their snow houses and greeted the newcomers with opened hands and every sign of welcome. A few minutes later Hall, on his sledge, rode into the village and found himself face to face with Innookpoozheejook. Hall accepted the Eskimos' invitation to move his camp to the village, and that evening he and his party slept close to the Kikerktarmiut.

Everyone in the village had relics of the lost expedition; Innookpoozheejook's snow house was filled with them. Hall was shown a silver spoon with an eel's head crest (Franklin's) that came from a place where white men had died. There were three sledges with runners made from the masts of a ship that sank off O'Reilly Island and, from the same ship, the lower half of a finely brass-mounted mahogany writing desk, now serving as a blubber tray. They had a pickle jar, complete with cork, from near the Peffer River and part of a boat found at Erebus Bay, the plank and ribs all complete and copper-fastened. There was a piece of copper, stamped in several places with a broad arrow; a fragment of a handkerchief from the tent at Terror Bay; a double-bladed knife with a bone handle; and two long, white beads.

Hall stayed a week in the village, listening to stories of the Franklin expedition. He heard tale after tale of the tent at Terror Bay. One of the Eskimos who had been there told him that in the tent were "blankets, bedding & a great many skeleton bones—the flesh all off, nothing except sinews attached to them—the appearance as though foxes & wolves had gnawed the flesh off the bones. Some bones had been severed with a saw. Some skulls with holes in them."

Hall heard about the ship at Ookjoolik with the body of the big man aboard, and about the tracks of four white men and a dog seen on the land near by. He heard about the five bodies on Keeuna and the one on Kungearklearu and the two near the Peffer River. He heard about the bodies and the boat found in the inlet west of Point Richardson, and about the explosion that blew the snow house to bits.

Innookpoozheejook, in 1861, had searched the coast from Terror Bay up to Erebus Bay. He told Hall that at Terror Bay he had seen very little—only the mark where the big tent had stood and near it three graves. At Erebus Bay, however, he had found the boat discovered by Hobson. About half a mile from it he found a second boat, clinker built and copper-fastened, also on a sledge. Probably because of the snow, Hobson and McClintock had missed this second boat. In it Innookpoozheejook had found a fully clothed skeleton and three skulls, also paddles and knives and forks and watches. There were a great many papers, too; but these the natives threw out and trampled underfoot. Alongside the boat was a pile of skeleton bones that had been broken open for marrow, and some knee-high boots with cooked human flesh in them.

In the village were Tutkeeta and Owwer, two of the natives who, twenty-one years before, had met the retreating white men near Cape Herschel. Twice Hall listened to their story. From the way it was told the first time, he believed that Tutkeeta and Owwer and the natives with them at the meeting "were noble, generous men, that they had contributed all they possibly could—indeed had given all the seal meat they had to Crozier & men. . . ." On hearing the story a second time, in a fuller and different version, it began to seem to him that the Eskimos had deliberately forsaken the white men. Why else had they packed up and left so early in the morning? He doubted Tutkeeta's statement that he and his companions did not at the time know "how very hungry they were, or they could have taken a few of the men to take care of them, to feed etc." With more certainty than ever, Hall felt he must now get to Tooshooarthariu. From him, Hall was sure, he would get at the truth in the conflicting Eskimo stories. Unhappily, Tooshooarthariu was not on Kikerktak, as Hall had been informed, but far away at Coronation Gulf.

A week passed; Hall's time began to run short. His natives were anxious to start back in two weeks. Soon, they said, the thaw would begin, the snow and ice would disappear from the shore of the Sea of Akkoolee (Committee Bay), and travel by sledge would be impossible. Hall insisted that he wanted to make a summer search on King William Island, to visit Terror Bay and Erebus Bay and go on up the coast to Crozier's landing place where, he had heard from Eskimos at Repulse Bay, the records of the expedition were buried. He could make the journey if one native would accompany him; not one volunteered. They were willing at most, in the two weeks that remained for traveling, to visit the mouth of the Peffer River, the Todd Islets, and the inlet west of Point Richardson. Hall left most of his party, including Joe and Hannah, behind at the snow-house village; with him he took Innookpoozheejook and an Eskimo, Jack, and his wife. On May 8, with one sledge and fourteen dogs, the party started westward; the thermometer read 30°, the sky was overcast, and snow falling.

By evening they had reached the southeast corner of King William Island. Hall, riding on the sledge, jotted in his note-book: "King William Land in sight the table-top-hill 'Matheson Isle.' 3 cheers I have just given. It is a glorious feeling time with me for 10 years have I been struggling to get to KWL . . ." On past midnight they traveled; by early morning they came to four snow houses occupied by four families.

In these snow houses were more Franklin relics—the lower half of an instrument box, a knife, a length of iron chain, a ten-inch bolt, a steel spearhead marked with the words THE SHIP, a silver fork with Franklin's crest, a glass jar, and a lead ball with a hole in it and a piece of skin running through the hole. When Hall asked where each one came from, its exact story was told him. The bolt came from a piece of wood picked up near Ookjoolik; the glass jar from a cask filled with such glass jars, found near where the ship went down; the lead ball from the boat in the inlet on the west side of Point Richardson.

Again Hall heard the stories he never tired of hearing. How Nukkeecheuk, on board the ship off O'Reilly Island, "looked all around, saw nobody & finally *Lik-lee-poo-nik-kee-look-oo-loo* (stole a very little or few things) & then made for the Ig-loos. Then all Innuits went to ship & stole a good deal—broke into a place that was fastened up & there found a very large white man who was dead, very tall man. There was flesh about this dead man, that is, his remains quite perfect—it took 5 men to lift him. The place smelt very bad. His clothes all on. Found dead on the floor—not in a sleeping place or berth." Again Hall heard about the tracks of the white men on the land not far from the ship, and about the tent at Terror Bay. One man told of having seen five graves on the island of Keeuna, and a skull and some bones lying about.

This man and his family, who were on their way to Ookjoolik, joined Hall's party, and two days later the whole group was encamped off Keeuna. Innookpoozheejook had abandoned all idea of going on to Point Richardson. As soon as Hall had visited Keeuna and the mouth of the Peffer River and Kungearklearu, the long, low spit of land where the body of the large man with the bad gums had been found, it would be time to start back. Already the thaw was setting in; the ice on the Sea of Akkoolee would soon be off the shores. Hall, resigned, wrote in one of his little notebooks: "I have 'untamable eagles' around me & must bend as the power is applied." A page or two later his mood had changed: "Notwithstanding the expressed anxiety of Innookpoozheejook, Jack & his wife to return soon as we have visited the graves of the 8 men of Franklin Expedition, I am determined if possible to continue on up to Terror Bay at least, if no farther, & visit the place where the large tent was in wh. so many of Franklin's men met their disasterous fate."

For four days, from Tuesday, May 11, to Saturday, May 15, Hall and his party camped by Keeuna. At the beginning of their stay Innookpoozheejook told Hall how Pooyetta found five bodies on the island, "each fully dressed—flesh all on the bones & unmutilated by any animals." He told of the two bodies found east of the Peffer River—"the remains facing upwards & the hands had been folded in a very precise manner across the breasts of both"—and of the body at Kungearklearu, it too with its hands crossed. Hall listened to every detail, then began his search.

On Keeuna he found only a piece of a human thigh bone, the joint-head of which had been badly gnawed by a fox. Innookpoozheejook assured him that the bone belonged to one of Franklin's men. East of the Peffer River he had better luck. There Innookpoozheejook located with a snow-prospecting staff one of the graves and laid bare a skeleton. Suddenly Hall felt in mystical communion with his heroes of the North. Were not these the remains, as he put it, of "one of those gallant sons of Franklin's Expedition that so triumphantly & gloriously accomplished the North West Passage?" He built a monument over the spot and raised two American flags at half-mast on a staff. He fired a salute of eight guns, one each for the eight Franklin men who had laid down their lives on the Todd Islands and on the nearby King William Island coast. He then disinterred the skeleton Innookpoozheejook had found, to return it to England. There, by a plug in a tooth, it was identified as that of Lieutenant Le Vesconte

of the *Erebus*. On Kungearklearu Hall found nothing. At the
spot where the grave was supposed to be he built a five-foot
monument and fired another eight-gun salute. Back at Keeuna,
Hall learned that the white men found on that island were
lying as they had died on top of the ground and that their
boots were made of leather. Late Friday afternoon the native
family that had accompanied Hall from the snow-house village went on their way to Ookjoolik. Saturday morning, after
building a monument on Keeuna and firing eight salutes, Hall
and his party started back. It was a beautiful day, warm and
bright, with the snow melting on the limestone strand.

There was sadness in Hall's heart and doubt in his mind.
He had come so far and had accomplished so little of what he
wanted to do. He had not been to Terror Bay or to Crozier's
landing place. He was uncertain now whether any of Franklin's men still lived. He had not met Tooshoorthariu, who
could have settled that point for him. He wanted once more
to hear Owwer's and Tutkeeta's story; careful questioning
might bring out the truth. Hall was no longer happily certain
about the kindliness of the Eskimos' feelings. Only four days
before he had been shocked by Innookpoozheejook's story of
two bodies being dug up at Terror Bay and knives stolen
from the graves. Of this incident, he wrote in his notebook:
"Innookpoozheejook very finicky to tell all the facts. No
Innuit before him to tell me about the Innuits digging up the
graves of the white men & leaving them unburied—in fact
telling how his race has dug up & robbed the dead of the
whites of everything buried with them."

On Sunday, May 16, Hall was back at the snow-house village. His own Eskimos were waiting there for him; the other
natives, Owwer and Tutkeeta among them, had left, with all

their belongings, for Boothia. They had probably gone as far as Shepherd Bay, where they would stop for sealing. On Monday Hall set out to find them. He wanted some of their Franklin relics to take home, and he wanted to talk with Owwer and Tutkeeta. At the head of Shepherd Bay he found their camp. Late that same day he was back at the snowhouse village. On his sledge he had the top half of a writing desk taken from the ship that went down near Ookjoolik. He had a piece of mast fourteen feet long from the same ship and a part of the boat found by Innookpoozheejook at Erebus Bay. With Hall were Owwer and Tutkeeta. He had brought them back that he might interview them with Hannah as interpreter.

On Tuesday, May 18, Owwer and Tutkeeta told their story again. It was almost the exact story they had told before, but with a few new details added. Again Hall heard about the meeting at the crack in the ice; how the white officer made the natives open their packs so that he could get the seal meat out; and how some of the white men slept in a big tent, side by side in two rows, and others slept in the boat. He waited for the ending; it would tell whether or not the natives had deserted starving men. As Owwer and Tutkeeta now told it, the Eskimos broke camp and hurried away, right past the white officer, who, as Hall wrote in his journal, *"tried to make them stop*—put his hand to his mouth and spoke the word 'Net-chuk' or 'Nest-chuck' (seal). But the Innuits were in a hurry—did not know the men were starving (A note I make here of my own conviction that the Innuits feel guilty of letting white men starve & thus their inconsistent stories. They deviate as no truth telling men.)" At the same interview Hall learned that Tooshoorothariu had never seen the white men again after the meeting near Cape Herschel. The story the Noowook natives had told him, of Tooshooarthariu's meeting Crozier and three other men and succoring them, was a fabrication from beginning to end.

Hall's disillusionment was complete. In his eyes Tooshooarthariu lost all Christian virtue; his companions became heartless heathens. In his notebook, in the belief that the officer in charge of the retreating men was Crozier, Hall, after hearing Owwer and Tutkeeta's story, made this entry: "These 4 families could have saved Crozier's life & that of his company had they been so disposed. They could have led them to their stores of freshly deposited seals that were along on the coast of K. W. Island—& could have sent word to the natives to contribute aid toward saving the starving men. But no, though noble Crozier plead with them, *they would not stop even a day* to try & catch seals—but early in the morning abandoned what they knew to be a large starving Company of white men. This a fact that I easily read in these men in my last 2 interviews with them." For such men and their race, all of whom were grave robbers as well, Hall had but one treatment: "*Civilize, enlighten* & Christianize them & their race. Then we shall have no more such sad history to hear & write."

On this note Hall ended his search. Owwer and Tutkeeta left; as a parting gift Hall gave to one an empty brandy bottle with a cork in it and to the other a half of an American tin can. Two days later, May 20, 1869 he and his party started for Repulse Bay; a month later they were there.

The North had refused Hall one of its prizes—Franklin survivors. His mind now turned to another prize—the North Pole. While he waited for a whaler to come to Repulse Bay, he read and reread the arctic books he had with him. "How my soul longs," he wrote, "for the time to come when I can be on my North Pole Expedition! I cannot, if I would, restrain my zeal for making Arctic discoveries. My purpose is to make as quick a voyage as possible to the States, and then, at once, make preparations for my Polar Expedition." On August 5 the *Ansell Gibbs*, of New Bedford, arrived. A few days later Hall was aboard, with Joe and Hannah and their adopted daughter, Punny. On the thirteenth the ship sailed; on September 26 she arrived at her home port.

Lady Franklin, when she heard of Hall's discoveries, wanted him to put off his polar voyage and go back to King William Island and look for the records. Hall refused. His expedition to the North Pole came first; after that he might go to King William Island again. He threw himself heart and soul into preparations for his new voyage of exploration. The following summer, 1870, Lady Franklin came to Cincinnati, still hopeful of changing Hall's mind, but nothing could shake him in his new purpose.

A year later, on July 29, 1871, Hall, aboard the *Polaris*, set out to discover the North Pole. With him went the faithful Joe and Hannah, glad to follow him to the ends of the earth. The ship sailed through Davis Strait, up Baffin Bay, and by the last day of August was in Smith Sound. On September 7, at latitude 81° 28′, the *Polaris* went into winter quarters. Two months later tragedy struck: on November 8, after a two weeks' illness, Hall died. He was buried ashore in his own beloved north, to lie forever in that strange, fascinating world of which he himself had once written: "The arctic region is my home, I love it dearly—its storms, its winds, its glaciers, its icebergs; and when I am among them, it seems as if I were in an earthly heaven, or a heavenly earth."

8.

At the bottom of the next search lay a silver Franklin spoon; it was cracked near where the handle joined the bowl, and the crack had been crudely mended with a bit of copper and two rivets. This mend marred the looks of the spoon, but made it easy to identify. About it there were three stories: Captain Barry's, Nutargeark's, and Captain Potter's.

Between 1871 and 1873 Captain Barry, while on a whaling expedition aboard the *Glacier*, had been frozen in, in Repulse Bay. When several Eskimos with their families visited the ship, Barry overheard them talking among themselves about a stranger in uniform who years before had come to their country—King William Island—with many other white men. These white men had all died, but not before they had built a cairn in which the chief had deposited many books and papers and some silver spoons. Barry found out where the cairn was, then proceeded to keep to himself what he had heard. He felt that it needed further substantiation.

This came three years later. Barry was then on the *A. Houghton*, before Marble Island; it was the winter of 1876. Again a party of Eskimos—different ones—visited the ship. This time, seeing the logbook, they said that a great white

223

man had once come among their people with just such a book. They then gave Barry a mended silver spoon, supposedly from the cairn where papers and books had been deposited. The spoon, it would seem, was all Barry needed to make him sure of his ground. On his return in 1877, he told the story of the cairn to the owners of his ship; they turned the facts over to Judge Daly, President of the American Geographical Society; and the spoon went on its way to Sir John Franklin's niece, Sophia Cracroft. The story of the find and a picture of the spoon appeared in the newspapers.

The story reached the ears of Lieutenant Frederick Schwatka of the Third United States Cavalry, who at once wanted to retrieve the records—obviously those of the Franklin expedition. To him it seemed a heaven-sent chance for romance and adventure. Judge Daly revealed to Schwatka all the facts in his possession, and Messrs. Morrison & Brown, with the help of public subscriptions, fitted out the *Eothen* to take the party north. With him Schwatka had William Gilder, a reporter for the *New York Herald;* Henry Klutschak, a civil engineer; Frank Melms, an experienced whaleman; and Hall's devoted Eskimo friend Joe, now a widower. They sailed from New York on June 19, 1878—thirty years and two months after the abandonment of the *Erebus* and the *Terror.* In command of the *Eothen* was none other than Captain Barry, whose story and whose spoon had prompted the expedition.

Seven weeks later, on August 7, the *Eothen* arrived at Depot Island off the west coast of Hudson Bay near the entrance to Roes Welcome; among the Eskimos coming to greet the ship was Papa, who had been to King William Island with Hall. The party made winter quarters at Camp Daly on the mainland just opposite Depot Island; in the spring they would start across the Barren Lands for the estuary of the Great Fish River. At once Schwatka began to track down what facts he could about the spoon. From the Eskimo Nutargeark he got a story that differed widely from Barry's.

Nutargeark said that he had brought from King William Island just such a spoon as Barry had recovered, with just such a mend as Schwatka described. It had come from one of the boat places or where skeletons had been found, either on King William Island or Adelaide Peninsula, he did not remember which. He had given the spoon to the wife of Sinuksook, a friend of his. She, he was sure, had given it not to Captain Barry but to Captain Potter. Sinuksook's wife, seen later, confirmed the story. There was, then, nothing to do but find Captain Potter.

Captain Potter turned out to be at Marble Island in command of the whaler *Abbie Bradford*. In January Gilder and Klutschak went down to see him. He had, he admitted, been with Barry on the *Glacier* in Repulse Bay. But he had no memory of Barry's getting a Franklin spoon while there. He had first heard about the spoon from the newspaper accounts published when the spoon was sent to Miss Cracroft. It was true that while he was on the *Glacier*, Sinuksook's wife had given him a spoon exactly like the Barry spoon, even to the mend. Strangely, the spoon disappeared shortly after he got it. Potter added that he gave short shrift to Barry's story about the cairn and the papers and the books. All Barry spoke was the pidgin English of the area, and with that it would be quite impossible to understand Eskimos talking among themselves. In short, Barry's whole story was ridiculous. "In this crucible of fact," the *New York Herald* reporter put it, "the famous spoon melted. So far as Captain Barry and his clews were concerned, we had come on a fool's errand."

Schwatka did not for a moment entertain the idea of turning back from King William Island. The spoon was a false clue. But no one had ever searched King William Island in summer; he might still be lucky enough to find the records. What was more, Nutargeark said that when the snow was off the ground many white men's skeletons could still be seen. Other things, too, not seen in winter might come to light in summer. His search, in a sense, would be complete and final; it would gather up the last loose ends of the Franklin mystery.

On April 1, 1879, the party left Camp Daly. There were four white men and thirteen Eskimos—men, women and children. The sledges carried a month's provisions and two weeks' food for the dogs—forty-two in all. When the provisions were gone the whole party would live off the land.

On May 15, halfway down the Hayes River, east of Chantrey Inlet, they met the first natives. Here a man of about sixty-five told how, as a boy, he had seen ten white men in a boat on the Great Fish River—Back's party, no doubt. The next white man he saw was a dead one in a ship frozen in the ice off Ookjoolik. He knew all about the ransacking of the ship, and he had himself seen the tracks of white men on the mainland. His son-in-law, Peowat, a man of forty, had apparently seen Chief Factor Anderson's two canoes, and had sometime later found a cairn on Montreal Island, from which he took a pocket knife, a pair of scissors, and some fishhooks. In all this lay hope for Schwatka. It was more than forty years since Back went down the river, thirty since the Franklin ship sank, and twenty-four since Anderson's expedition; yet all these events were still remembered clearly. Late as he was in his search, he was apparently not too late to find out facts not known before.

Schwatka went to Montreal Island and spent a day looking for Peowat's cairn, but with no luck. He then cut across Point Ogle, and on May 31 came to an Eskimo village in the bay just west of Point Richardson. There he heard of an inlet three or four miles away where books and papers had been found, a boat, and some dead Kabloonas. The next day he visited it and named the spot Starvation Cove. He had found the last camping place of the retreating crews; its exact location had taken thirty-one years to discover. "No more powerful picture of utter abandonment could possibly be devised than this," wrote Gilder, the *New York Herald* correspondent. "The land low and barren, so low, indeed, as to be scarcely distinguished from the sea, as both lay covered with their mantle of snow. Neither tree nor sprout, and scarcely a hill visible—nothing whatever to relieve the crushing monotony of the scene—no living thing to be seen anywhere, though the eye had uninterrupted range over so vast a territory." At the time snow made searching impossible; a later search brought to light a pewter medal that commemorated the launching of the steamer *Great Britain* in 1843, and, among some seaweed, a few pieces of blanket and a skull.

The evening of the day Schwatka found Starvation Cove he had the good luck to meet Ahlangyah, who had seen the retreating Franklin party on the east coast of Washington Bay. One of them had given her husband a chopping knife. What impressed her most deeply about the white men was that their mouths were dry and black and hard, and that none of them wore fur clothing.

Three days later a native told Schwatka that he, during the

previous summer, had found a new white man's cairn near the Peffer River on King William Island; one never before seen by Eskimos. Near it were three graves and a tent place, where he had picked up a pair of wire gauze snow goggles. With the native as guide Schwatka and Gilder took a light sledge and their own driver, Toolooah, and crossed over Simpson Strait to the spot, twenty-five miles away. The cairn was there, but it was the one built by Hall. On one side of a stone he had scratched H MAY XII 1869 and on the other ETERNAL HONOR TO THE DISCOVERERS OF THE NORTH WE—. The remaining letters had been broken off.

Schwatka returned to Adelaide Peninsula, and there he spoke with an old woman, Tooktoocheer. She was none other than Pooyetta's wife, and her son, Ogzeuckjeuwock, was with her. It was he who, as a child of twelve, had blown up the snow house in the inlet west of Point Richardson; now forty-two, he was a successful medicine man. The old woman, in her seventies and with a failing memory, sat by and nodded while her son did most of the talking. The explosion, of course, he remembered; also seeing a boat and skulls and bones. And he remembered a sealed or locked tin box, about two feet long and a foot square. This his father and friends broke open and found full of books; they dumped them on the ground and left them. These books, Schwatka was sure, were the valuable records of the expedition, carried to the end in their tin box.

On June 10 the party crossed from Point Seaforth on Adelaide Peninsula to Point Gladman on King William Island, and two days later they were at Cape Herschel. There Joe and many of the natives stayed. The four white men, with Toolooah and his wife and child and the other Eskimo, took a dog team and sledge and started north. From the head of Washington Bay they went overland to Erebus Bay and on up the coast to Cape Felix; they would come back to Erebus Bay again when the ground was completely bare. Not for twenty years—not since McClintock and Hobson—had white men been along this coast. In that time, no doubt, the elements and the natives had taken their toll of the Franklin relics; Schwatka was determined to find whatever was left.

At Crozier's landing place, still strewn on the shore, were cooking stoves and copper kettles and blankets and clothing and implements of one kind and another. A little eastward of the ruins of the cairn, Schwatka's party found an open grave with a few bones lying scattered around it. In the grave itself was a skull, resting on a neatly folded handkerchief of figured silk, still almost perfectly preserved. There were gilt buttons, too, and rotting blue cloth, and a quantity of canvas with coarse stitching through it, as if the body had been sewn up for burial at sea. The gilt buttons and the fineness of the cloth left little doubt that the body was that of an officer. On a stone at the foot of the grave lay a medal, thickly covered with mud. When cleaned off it was made out to be the second prize in mathematics, awarded in midsummer 1830 by the Royal Naval College to John Irving. This identified the grave as that of Lieutenant John Irving, third officer of the *Terror* and, at the time of his death, officer in charge of the party returning to the ships from Terror Bay.

On July 3 Schwatka made his most northerly camp three miles below Cape Felix, where the Franklin men had pitched their three tents in the summer of 1847. Of the many relics found at this spot by Hobson in 1859, all that was left was "what appeared to be a torn-down cairn, and a quantity of canvas and coarse red woollen stuff, pieces of blue cloth, broken bottles, and other similar stuff, showing that there had been a permanent camping place here from the vessels, while a piece of an ornamented china tea-cup, and cans of preserved potatoes showed that it was in charge of an officer."

A search of Cape Felix disclosed on a high hill two miles inland a seven-foot cairn, the work of white men. Schwatka carefully took it down stone by stone to find it empty. "It seemed unfortunate," wrote Gilder, "that probably the only cairn left standing on King William Land, built by the hands of white men, should have had no record left in it." . . . From its emptiness Schwatka inferred that the cairn had been used for scientific purposes or for determining the drift of the ships. The next day he and his men rebuilt the cairn and put in it a record of their own work.

On July 7 Schwatka left Cape Felix for Crozier's landing place, to search it again now that the snow was going. Near Wall Bay he came upon another cairn—one that for a moment held the promise of a lucky discovery. The top of the cairn had been taken down, "but in the first course of stones, covered and protected by those thrown from the top, he found a piece of paper with a carefully drawn hand upon it, the index finger pointing at the time in a southerly direction." On the hidden end of the paper might there not be a message? Schwatka quickly removed the stone to look; there was no other end to the paper, it had completely rotted away. Below Cape Maria Louisa he found an Eskimo cache in which, among other things, were a tin powder can, a small keg, and several red tins marked GOLDNER'S PATENT—preserved meat tins from the *Erebus* and *Terror*.

Back at Crozier's landing place on July 11, the party found the ground bare of snow. Searching was easy, and many different articles were lying around: "a brush with the name 'H. Wilks' cut in the side, a two-gallon stone jug stamped 'R. Wheatley, wine and spirit merchant, Greenhithe, Kent,' several tin cans, a pickle bottle, a canvas pulling strap, a sledge harness marked with a stencil plate 'T 11,' showing it to have belonged to the *Terror*." In among the ruins of the cairn Toolooah's wife picked up a paper. Hope was high that it might be some further message from Crozier. But it was only a copy, in McClintock's handwriting, of the original record found by Hobson. Schwatka, who on his previous visit had gathered up Lieutenant Irving's remains to send them back to England, now built over the lonely grave a monument of stone. Then the party moved on down the coast.

Between Collinson Inlet and Franklin Point they buried parts of a skull found on the way up. Fifteen miles south of Franklin Point was an officer's grave, with the telltale gilt buttons and fine linen and cloth. The grave was on top of a little hillock of sand and gravel, where burial beneath the ground was possible. The natives had opened the grave, but the earth, where it had been carefully rounded up, still showed; everywhere about the grave, and even in it, a mass of tiny wild flowers grew—little purple willow herbs, daisies, and creamy white dryas. Schwatka reburied the scattered bones and marked the grave; then, as a remembrance to take home, he picked a handful of the tiny flowers. Four miles farther on was another grave; it had been stripped of everything but a brass buckle and a percussion cap. A quarter of a mile away a skull lay on the beach. All along the stretch of coast from Franklin Point to Erebus Bay, tenting places of white men marked the slowness of the tragic retreat.

At the bottom of each of the many inlets on the south side of Erebus Bay, Schwatka found pieces of navy blue cloth, washed up by the rising tides. On the shore of the inlet where the camp had been he came upon the wreck of a boat. Strewn on the shore still were fishing lines, bullets, canvas, clothing, the drag rope of a sledge, broken medicine bottles and a lantern—the lantern carried, no doubt, against the time when, farther south and later in the season, the nights would be dark. At this camp Schwatka found and buried the partial remains of four skeletons.

On July 24, while Schwatka and his men were still at Erebus Bay, the ice broke up. The sledge became useless, and the party, in short stages, packed everything, including two Franklin stoves, across the narrow neck of land to Terror Bay, which they reached on August 3. There Schwatka and Gilder stayed; the others went east to Cape Herschel and Gladman Point. Terror Bay was barren of relics; not a trace remained of the many bodies that had lain dead in the tent. The stones that marked the tent site were gone; no graves showed. The sea had washed the beach clean; it was as if not even a single white man had ever been to the spot. On the coast to the west, between Terror Bay and Cape Crozier, Schwatka found one skeleton—the only one ever found on Gore Peninsula.

Later, at Tulloch Point, some twenty-five miles east of Cape Herschel, he found seventeen bones of a skeleton. The grave in which they lay was sketchily made of small stones, though larger and more suitable ones were near by. The larger stones had probably been too heavy for the weakened men to lift.

Shortly after the middle of September Schwatka went into camp at the narrows of Simpson Strait, not far from Malerualik—the place where the caribou cross. Winter was setting in; the lakes were freezing over and the season of snow was at hand. Every day immense herds of caribou were seen. One day Schwatka's party alone killed twenty-six. On October 1 the ice on the strait was thick enough for the animals to cross to the continent; thereafter their numbers rapidly decreased, until two weeks later there were none at all left on Kikerktak. The weather got steadily colder; the mean temperature for October was zero, with a low of −38°.

On November 8 Schwatka left King William Island. He ordered two sledges to go directly to the Great Fish River, while he and Gilder, with a third sledge, went around the west side of Adelaide Peninsula to Grant Point and Sherman Inlet, and eventually on to join the others above the Dangerous Rapids. Near the mouth of Sherman Inlet Schwatka found his last relics of the Franklin men. Natives there still had a piece of one of the boats from the ship that sank near O'Reilly Island and a part of a block from the same ship. And through the years, while papers and records from the expedition rotted away, these natives had treasured a piece of an old wax candle. A day or two farther on he met four Eskimo women on a sledge. One of them, an aged crone, had, when a young woman, seen white men on Boothia and had been with Pooyetta when he found the boat and skeletons in Starvation Cove. After hearing her story, Schwatka left behind him for good and all the trail of the Franklin men.

On December 5 he reached the Great Fish River, and the rest of the party joined him there a few days later. The homeward journey was long and bitterly cold. The party followed the river up nearly to Mount Meadowbank, where, on the last day of the year, they struck out across the Barren Lands. On January 3, at five o'clock in the afternoon, the temperature stood at −71°. During the entire month the weather was so stormy that they could travel but eleven days, and February was the same. Their seal blubber ran low; they had barely enough for lighting the snow houses—none at all for warmth or cooking. They ate their meat so hard frozen that it had to be cut into convenient-sized lumps with a saw. Hardly a day passed but one of the dogs died; the men were always in the harness. On March 4 they reached Camp Daly, after a round-trip journey of 3,251 miles. As far as the records of the Franklin expedition were concerned, they had come back empty-handed; but no one before them had made so thorough and complete a search of Kikerktak.

PART IV
The Island Today

1.

With Schwatka the three great searches on King
William Island came to an end. For twenty-five years—ever
since Rae's report in 1854—the island had been in the world's
limelight, not as Kikerktak but as the scene of the Franklin
disaster. Hobson and McClintock had found it bleak and
desolate; Hall had seen it as the home of heathen inhabitants
who had knowingly left starving men to die. Schwatka, there
in the summer, had caught a glimpse of its beauty and loveli-
ness, but for him the pity and horror of the Franklin story
had been supreme. Could Kikerktak, the island of long ago,
with its stories of giants and giant-killers, ever be believed in
again?

Twenty-four years passed; no white men visited the island.
Then, in September 1903, they came again; this time from
Norway. They were seven in number, and they were in the
47-ton *Gjoa*—a reconditioned herring boat with a 13-horse-
power auxiliary motor. They had left Norway barely three
months before, not on a Franklin search but on their way
through the Northwest Passage: Amundsen was making a
boyhood dream come true. He had touched at Beechey Island,
then followed on the path of the *Erebus* and the *Terror*

through Barrow Strait and Peel Sound and into Franklin Strait. From Franklin Strait he went down the east side of King William Island; he found Simpson Strait completely open. For his scientific observations Amundsen needed to be some ninety miles from the Magnetic Pole, where the inclination of the dipping needle would be about 89°. He needed, too, a safe harbor for his ship. He found the spot he wanted on the island's southeast coast, twenty-five miles from Mount Matheson. It was, as one of the expedition put it, "the finest little harbour in the world"; it was small and quite sheltered from the winds—an ideal place to winter. On September 9 Amundsen explored it in a rowboat and pronounced it perfect in every way: "The shore around the harbour was very low, sandy moss-clad ground, gradually rising to a height of about 160 feet. Two little streams provided fresh water; if these dried up, as seemed probable, there was, right on the crest of the ridge, a fairly large pond containing drinkable water. A number of cairns and tent circles showed that Eskimo had been there, but that, of course, might have been a long time ago." The next day a large herd of caribou and many birds were seen. There was no iron in the rocks and stones—nothing to interfere with his magnetic observations. On Saturday, September 12, the prevailing north wind died down, and Amundsen's vessel, under her own power, entered the little harbor, which thereupon took the name Gjoa Haven. Provisions and explosives were put ashore; a magnetic station was built of forty copper-nailed wooden cases filled with sand. Later a second house of sixty cases was added as living quarters for two members of the expedition. For the next two years there were white men on Kikerktak.

Late in October five Eskimos visited the ship. They had known that white men were on the island, but gunfire had frightened them and kept them away. They gained courage as time went on and risked a meeting. Amundsen was struck by their appearances—handsome and tall and muscular; two of them not at all unlike what he pictured American Indians to be. They stayed overnight, then went home. A couple of days later they were back, bringing some dressed skins. Amundsen accompanied them home to their camp, near a large lake some twelve miles down the coast to the west. They came within sight of the camp at dusk, and looking down from a ridge into a little valley Amundsen saw six snow houses, each glowing with its own light, the rays of which "filtered through the ice windows of the huts, out into the last faint dusky-green shimmer of fading daylight in the west." At the sound of the word "Kabloona" the inhabitants rushed out and sur-rounded him. They stared at his face and at his clothes and felt him and stroked him, almost as if to make certain he was real.

The Eskimo visits to the ship became frequent; often they built snow houses and stayed for many days. The visiting continued until just before Christmas. On Christmas Day one of the Eskimos, Teraiu, came on board with a sad tale to tell. The rest of the tribe had gone away and left him and his wife and child behind. They would starve, he said, unless Amund-sen allowed them to build a snow house near the ship for the winter. A week later Teraiu and his family moved in. Teraiu liked best to sit outside the mess room and watch the cooking. He and his son got used to the white men's food, but his wife stayed loyal to raw meat and raw fish. Every morning Teraiu gave lessons in the art of building snow houses; always he was full of fun and helpfulness. It was this that saved him two months later, when the truth behind his move came to light. His tribe had never abandoned him; he had stayed behind by choice. Far from facing starvation, he had carefully hidden away six caribou carcasses. All he had wanted was to spend the winter with the Kabloonas.

On March 1 Amundsen and a small party set out for the Magnetic Pole, but the cold was so extreme that on the third day they had to turn back. Two weeks later he tried again. Already he was copying the Eskimo way of doing things. He found their clothing superior to European dress. Of sledge runners he wrote: "One can't do better in these matters than copy the Eskimo, and let the runners get a fine covering of ice; then they slide like butter." He gave up treating frostbites with snow; no Eskimo ever did that. Instead he touched the spot with a warm hand until the blood came back again. He had not yet "gone native" so far as Hall did, but he was fast learning how to be as happy and comfortable as the natives around him.

On the sea ice south of Matty Island, almost precisely where McClintock had met Eskimos, Amundsen met them, too—thirty-four men and boys out sealing. Among them was Atikleura, who at once caught Amundsen's eye: "A fine fellow he was, with raven black hair, and unlike his fellow tribesmen, he had a luxuriant growth of beard; he was broad shouldered and somewhat inclined to corpulency." Everything about him was superior and choice—his clothes, his dogs, and his tackle. Later, at the Eskimo village of sixteen snow houses, Amundsen visited Atikleura, who presented him with a fine suit of reindeer skins. When Amundsen hinted that he would like some underclothes as well, there was not a minute's hesitation on the part of Atikleura. He undressed, took off his own underwear and handed it to Amundsen. With no choice but to put it on at once, Amundsen, considerably embarrassed by the presence of Atikleura and his wife, redressed from the skin out, hiding himself as best he could with some of the bedclothes on the sleeping platform. A little beyond Atikleura's camp Amundsen turned back from his second effort to reach the Magnetic Pole. On the return journey he stopped again for a night at the native village, and had the good fortune, the next day, to watch the villagers break camp. The sight of the Kikerktarmiut on the move deeply impressed him: "In all there were nine sledges, to which both men and dogs were harnessed. Many of the women were employed as draught animals, and smart they were, too, and a pleasure to look at." Two days later he was back at Gjoa Haven. After eleven days he started again for the Magnetic Pole, which he reached the first week in May.

At the end of the month the *Gjoa* was still buried in snow, with drifts reaching halfway up her masts. In June the ice in the harbor was twelve and a half feet thick. Eskimos came in great numbers and put up their snow houses around the ship; later they moved to tents overlooking the nearby lakes, where they could fish and watch for the returning caribou. After the middle of June the smaller lakes began to break up; the ridgetops lost their snow; everywhere were ducks and swans and loons. Soon the temperature was in the high seventies, and, as Amundsen put it, "the flowers and herbs were now sprouting, and millions of insects hummed and buzzed and fussed busily around us after their long torpor." Kikerktak had come to life again in all its summer beauty. The discovery of a whale's skeleton, with its vertebrae projecting from an inland ridge, was remindful of the island's slow rise from the sea. There were days of fishing and visiting with the natives. By the middle of July the ice in Simpson Strait had turned to a bright bluish-green; it would soon be breaking up. A month later all the natives had left Gjoa Haven, and on August 16 there was rain and sleet; it was so cold that a fire was welcome.

On October 23 Amundsen left for a lake to the south of Point Richardson; he wanted to visit a large Eskimo encampment reported to be on the lake, and he hoped to be able to barter for a supply of fish. The ground was already covered with snow, Simpson Strait was frozen over, and the temperature was −13°. After two days of traveling he was at his destination, disappointed to find the camp much smaller than he had expected—only ten snow houses. It was situated not far from the bottom of Starvation Cove—a bleak enough place in winter, Amundsen admitted. But "there when summer comes," he wrote, "and millions of flowers brighten up the fields: there where all the waters gleam and all the ponds sing and bubble during the short freedom from the yoke of ice: there where the birds swarm and brood with a thousand glad notes and the first buck stretches his head over the ice harbour: there a heap of bleached skeletons marks the spot where the remains of Franklin's brave crowd drew their last breath in the last act of that sad tragedy." He and his party stayed at the Eskimo encampment only a few days. They had struck a good bargain, and they started back for Gjoa Haven with their sledge loaded with cod. On the way they passed by Keeuna, where Teraiu pointed out a large white stone that had been set up in memory of dead Franklin men.

The second winter was little different from the first; a little milder, perhaps. A census showed eighteen native families—sixty persons in all—at or near Gjoa Haven. In sheer numbers they were a threat, should they wish to cause trouble for the seven white men, and Amundsen devised an ingenious way of impressing them with his power. He built a snow house not far from the ship, and in it put a mine with a train leading to it under the snow. He then called the Eskimos aboard and lectured them on what the white men could do if trouble broke out anywhere—for instance, over there at that snow house. With these words, there was a shattering explosion, clouds of snow flew high into the air, and the house was gone. The Eskimos were duly impressed; perhaps behind their sober looks were thoughts of another igloo blown up by black sand stuff that dead white men had left behind. To help pass the time, the party formed a society to taste all the products of the land. Fox steak was judged delicious, and caribou tripe not bad.

At the end of the second winter the natives began to talk about the Franklin expedition. They knew but a little. They had heard of the ship that went down off Ookjoolik: how wood and iron had been got from her, and how a few people had eaten something out of tins and were later sick, and died. Of the second ship they knew nothing at all. An interpreter might have found out more, but there was none aboard the *Gjoa;* the only Eskimo spoken was what Amundsen and his men had picked up.

On the last day of July, 1905, the ice in Simpson Strait began to move, and on the 13th of August the *Gjoa* sailed. Just as the sun was setting she passed Hall Point near the Peffer River. The year before, members of the expedition had found the skeletons of two white men lying on top of the ground there. They had buried them and marked the site with a cairn. Now, "with our colours flying in honour of the dead we went by the grave in solemn silence; the sky and the land then glowing with a soft red, golden light." The *Gjoa* sailed on through Simpson Strait and to the west; after a third winter in the ice off King Point, she reached Bering Strait. Amundsen had made his childhood dream of sailing the Northwest Passage come true.

Eighteen more years passed and no white explorers came to Kikerktak. What was there to bring them? The Franklin mystery was solved; the Northwest Passage had been sailed through. Then, on June 13, 1923, came Knud Rasmussen. He was on a unique journey along the arctic coast, not by boat, but by sledge; not for geographical discovery, but to learn about the Eskimos themselves. The son of a Danish missionary and his part Eskimo wife, he had been born at Jakobshaven at the head of Disco Bay in Greenland, 165 miles north of the Arctic Circle. His first language was Eskimo, and as far back as he could remember, the myths and legends of the natives had fascinated him. At twelve he left home to go to school in Denmark, and at twenty-one, in 1900, he entered the University of Copenhagen. But his heart was in the North, and two years later he was back in his native land on an expedition to Melville Bay, where he first met the Polar Eskimos. He saw how dependent they had become on Peary's expeditions and the occasional whaler for foreign supplies—especially for guns and ammunition; and how, when these sources failed, they were threatened with starvation. In 1910 he founded at Thule the most northerly trading post in the world. The more he saw of the Polar Eskimos, the more their culture fascinated him. He longed to trace it back to its beginnings. Where had these people come from? Would not a visit to all the tribes along the arctic coast be the best way to find out? On March 11, 1923 he left Repulse Bay and headed for Bering Strait by sledge. With him he had two of his beloved Polar Eskimos— a young man and a young woman, not husband and wife, but cousins.

He sledged up the North Pole River and across Rae Isthmus and on to Pelly Bay, where he met an old man named Iggiararjuk, whose father had seen some of the Franklin men.

Now, seventy-five years after the event, Iggiararjuk told Rasmussen what had happened:

> My father Mangaq was with Tetqatsaq and Qablut on a seal hunt on the west side of King William's Land when they heard shouts, and discovered three white men who stood on shore waving to them. This was in the spring; there was already open water along the land, and it was not possible to get in to them before low tide. The white men were very thin, hollow-cheeked, and looked ill. They were dressed in white man's clothes, had no dogs and were traveling with sledges which they drew themselves. They bought seal meat and blubber, and paid with a knife. There was great joy on both sides at this bargain, and the white men cooked the meat at once with the aid of the blubber, and ate it. Later on the strangers went along to my father's tent camp and stayed there the night before returning to their own little tent, which was not of animal skins but of something that was white like snow. At that time there were already caribou on King William's Land, but the strangers only seemed to hunt wildfowl; in particular there were many eider ducks and ptarmigan then. The earth was not yet alive and the swans had not come to the country. Father and his people would willingly have helped the white men, but could not understand them; they tried to explain themselves by signs, and in fact learned to know a lot by this means. They had once been many, they said; now they were only few, and they had left their ship out in the pack-ice. They pointed to the south, and it was understood that they wanted to go home overland. They were not met again, and no one knows where they went to.

From Pelly Bay Rasmussen crossed to the west side of Boothia and started out on to Shepherd Bay. Near where Hall had met natives he came to an Eskimo village. It was early in May; already he had been two months on the way. The natives were busy sealing; it was no time to interrupt them; he could see them later in the summer on King William Island.

He went on up toward the North Magnetic Pole to study the natives there, and late in May he was back in Shepherd Bay again. By now he had collected a good many ethnological specimens which he felt should be sent, for safekeeping, to the nearest Hudson's Bay Post, on the west side of Kent Peninsula. He decided to send Qavigarrsuaq—the Polar Eskimo—on to the post with the collection. On his return Qavigarrsuaq could bring back a much needed supply of ammunition. The natives had many more guns than Rasmussen had expected; it was hard to be among them and not help out with powder and shot. As a result Rasmussen had cut deeply into his own supply, and it would soon be running short. Qavigarrsuaq, however, could bring back enough for everyone. On May 5 he left for Kent Peninsula; he would meet Rasmussen in about a month at Malerualik on King William Island.

Meanwhile Rasmussen went first to the mouth of the Great Fish River and then on up to Franklin Lake, where he met the same tribe of natives that Back had seen. In their tradition Back and his party were remembered as "smiling men, who walked with lumps of wood in their mouths emitting smoke." They were spoken of, too, as being dangerous and easily angered—men, in other words, to be afraid of. Rasmussen stayed among these people for over a month, and on June 13 he was on King William Island at Malerualik, where he had agreed to meet Qavigarrsuaq.

There was, however, no sign of the Eskimo, nor did he show up in the weeks immediately following. Rasmussen waited patiently. He had other natives with him, and he settled down to excavate a ruined village of stone houses that he had found a short distance from his camp. Spring was at its loveliest on Kikerktak. The last patches of snow were going;

tiny flowers were coming out everywhere; and on all the little lakes—the first to melt—were ducks and geese and eider ducks. The swamps were full of wading birds, and the drier stretches of the tundra, like meadows, were already turning a sappy green. A scorching sun shone out of a clear sky, and over the whole scene, as over an enchanted land where something wonderful might at any moment happen, hung a delicate blue haze.

Still Qavigarrsuaq did not appear, nor did any word come from him. Rasmussen, with his trading goods used up and his ammunition nearly gone, was in the position of a man without ready cash. Any specimens he wanted, any work he wanted done, he had to pay for with a promise against the day of Qavigarrsuaq's return. It was a fine time to gather folklore; the natives were more than willing to tell him their stories for nothing. But when Rasmussen wrote the stories down, then they were something he would take away with him, and as such, like other things to be taken away, were to be paid for. All he had for payment was promises of goods yet to come. He himself had no tobacco or coffee or tea or sugar—he had just a little saccharin, which he used to sweeten a tasteless drink brewed from a local herb. One of the natives made a mold out of soapstone, and by means of it Rasmussen was able to cast his shot into bullets. By the end of the first week in July all the natives had moved on to the inland lakes, where trout fishing would soon begin. Rasmussen and his helpers stayed behind to get on with the excavating and to be where he had agreed to meet Qavigarrsuaq. Game was scarce, it was the wrong time of year for hunting. A net set in the nearby river caught a few salmon, but never enough to keep the dogs in food. If the team were to be fed, it would be necessary to leave Malerualik and go elsewhere. On July 25 the party moved. There were eight people in all and seventeen dogs, each animal carrying a pack-saddle load of fifty pounds or more. The party was bound for Amitsoq across the inland plains.

Summer was nearly over; rain fell almost continuously; chilling fogs blew in from the sea and temperatures fell nearly to freezing. The first day of hunting brought Rasmussen's party five caribou; they spent the next two days in camp, taking care of the dogs and feeding them back to condition. Slowly the party moved northward—across bogs and around lakes and over a country that seemed endlessly flat. They ran into a flock of molting geese, unable to fly, a few of which, with the help of the dogs, they were able to catch. Another day they came upon a cache of caribou meat, at least more than one winter and one summer old. Its age, by the law of the land, made it theirs for the taking. The meat was green with mold and full of maggots; the natives scooped it up by the handful and ate it with relish. The first of August was lovely and clear, a warm day that ended with a blood-red sunset—a sign that an old man or an old woman had died. On the 5th of August they reached Amitsoq—the place where the spirits felt kindly toward men.

It was still early in the season; the good fishing had not yet begun. The native encampment was small, only five tents and not more than thirty persons in all. The daily catch amounted to some two dozen trout; later the fishing would be so good that each family could count on taking between 1,500 and 2,000 pounds in a fortnight. The day Rasmussen arrived was clear and hot, one of the days on which the Kikerktarmiut relax and dream. He saw them at their happiest and their best, carefree and full of fun, without a worry in the world. For the moment they seemed to forget that they lived in a land where food was often far from plenty, where starvation always lurked. Gay little children ran around naked in the sunshine and bathed in the lake. The older people played games and visited and laughed. Rasmussen mingled with them and heard their stories and their legends, and marveled that they managed to live at all in so barren and bleak a land.

Rasmussen stayed a week at Amitsoq. By the 17th of August he was back at Malerualik. Qavigarrsuaq was not there. Could it be that he was not coming at all? By now he was two months overdue, and Rasmussen was worried. His own ammunition was dangerously low; he had rationed his matches to two a day.

Autumn set in; cold weather began to come. Rasmussen built himself a stone house with turf-covered walls. The evening he finished the house visitors came, and there was talk of Qavigarrsuaq; why had he not come back? The natives were certain that he was dead, probably killed by unfriendly people along the way. What else could account for his not showing up? Rasmussen's plight touched them; they knew what it was to lose a friend and what it was to have supplies run short. When they left, each gave him a piece of tobacco—some of the same tobacco they had bought from the white man when they first met.

Three days later Qavigarrsuaq's cousin saw, out in Simpson Strait beyond a distant flat point, something dark on the water. She pointed it out to Rasmussen. In a moment he had his glasses on it; it was a tiny canoe with two men. In another hour Qavigarrsuaq and a companion had arrived, and the whole camp rushed down to meet them. At last there would be enough ammunition. Rasmussen would make good on all his promises; the day that everyone was waiting for had come.

But Qavigarrsuaq had a sorry tale to tell. Heavy going and

hostile natives had delayed him on his journey to Kent Peninsula. He had delivered the collection safely. On the way back in June the rivers had broken up; he had had to abandon his sledge and borrow a canoe and wait for the ice to clear out before he could paddle along the coast. He had brought Rasmussen no ammunition or supplies. It had been a good year for fox skins; the Hudson's Bay Post was traded out.

Rasmussen had hardly expected such an outcome. Without more ammunition it would be all but impossible to keep his dogs alive; without his dogs there would be little chance of his continuing his journey to Bering Strait. Also, without goods, how was he to redeem his promises to the natives? For food his only hope was the migrating caribou. They would soon be passing by Malerualik on their way to the continent. His ammunition was down to seventy-five rounds; if he used it sparingly, perhaps he could get enough meat to carry on for a while. Suddenly he found himself waiting for the caribou at Malerualik, just as down through the ages the Kikerktarmiut had always waited for them there.

On September 15 the caribou came. They poured out of the hills and down over the ridges to the shore, where they were met by a burst of native rifle fire. For a moment the animals were dazed. Then, in bewilderment, the cavalcade broke up into small groups which galloped back to the safety of the interior, there to wait until fear left them, when again they would try to cross the strait.

Rasmussen and Qavigarrsuaq took no part in the hunt. They were afraid that in the excitement of the moment they might shoot wildly and waste ammunition. Three days later they went inland and there shot seven fat caribou, which, unskinned, they brought back to camp on their sledge. Temporarily, the dogs could be taken care of. But still Rasmussen was troubled by his promised payments to the Eskimos.

On September 21 there was a great stir in the native encampment. Men and women and children rushed out of their tents, surprise on every face. For a moment they looked out across the strait, as if seeing a sight they couldn't believe: a great white spirit or a huge bird with widespread white wings was coming across the water. They hurried to Rasmussen and pointed it out. Relief had arrived. He did not know what little ship it was or why it had come; but it would certainly have ammunition on board. He could now pay off his debts and keep his dog team alive. The little ship—a 20-ton sailing vessel—anchored off Malerualik, and two men came ashore in a motor boat. They were Peter Norberg and Henry Bjorn and were on their way to open a Hudson's Bay Post on King William Island. They had aboard all the ammunition anyone could want, and plenty of other supplies, too. For Rasmussen the day was saved; on November 1 he would be on his way to Nome to complete the Northwest Passage by sledge. For the Kikerktarmiut the arrival of the ship was the end of a long history that began with the driving out of the Tunrit. Now the first white settlers had come; from that day on the island would never again be entirely the islanders'.

Through the years King William Island has slowly changed with the rest of the changing North. The Hudson's Bay Company's first post—a small sheet-iron store and a double canvas house—went up not far from Malerualik. In 1926 this post moved to Gjoa Haven, where it has been ever since. At Gjoa Haven, too, the Canalaska Trading Company established a post. In 1936 they closed their station, and the Catholic Mission took over the buildings. At Terror Bay another post, with a permanent house, was built by an independent trader. The house has long been abandoned and is now, in winter, sometimes used by natives trapping on the west coast. But all summer long it stands empty and alone on a low limestone point—in front of it the clear blue waters of the bay, and behind it the mirrorlike lagoons and the sheltering ridges beyond. It is a reminder that not only Franklin's men have lived with the beauty and enchantment of this spot.

On King William Island the Franklin search has never come to an end. More bones and more skulls have been found; and there have come to light a story and a map, purporting to tell where Franklin and the expedition records are buried. The story came from an old sea captain in Alaska, Peter Bayne, one of the five white men hired from the whalers by Hall in 1867. Bayne heard it from Boothian natives at Repulse Bay, and always hoped to investigate it himself, but the chance never came. The first summer the *Erebus* and the *Terror* were off Cape Felix, so the natives' story went, men came ashore and put up a camp of one big tent and some small ones. At this camp men sickened and died and were buried on the south side of a nearby ridge. Then, one day, a body was brought from the ships and buried there too, not in the ground like the other bodies, but in an opening in the rock, where it was covered with something that "after a while was all same stone." The man must have been a person of importance, for at his burial many guns were fired. Could it have been Franklin? After all these years, was his grave to be found? Another part of the story told of papers in cemented vaults at the same place.

The map shows a point named Victory Point. Marked on it are a cairn near the point's tip, a little inland from the cairn a camp, and farther back still, on the south side of the ridge, five graves. In 1930 a Canadian Government party flew to the area to check on the story and the map. They searched the coast northward from Crozier's landing place to Ross's Victory Point; nowhere did they find signs of a cemented grave or cemented vaults. That they failed to find the grave is not surprising. At the time of Franklin's death the *Erebus* and the *Terror* were northwest of Cape Felix. It seems highly improbable that his body would have been taken the long distance south to Victory Point for burial. It looked as if the story were a hoax.

There remained the chance that the map might be of some other point, wrongly marked Victory Point. But where? A recent air photograph is suggestive. The photograph shows, south of Cape Felix, a stretch of coast and a point surprisingly like those on the map. The point is where the Franklin men had their summer camp in 1847, where there certainly were tents and a big cairn. Could this be where Franklin's body has lain undiscovered for over a hundred years? Against the possibility is the fact that both Hobson and Schwatka thoroughly searched the spot; it is hard to believe that they would have missed anything. On the other hand, neither of them had ever heard of Bayne's story; neither of them was looking for a grave in an opening in a rock, covered over with cement.

And what of the Kikerktarmiut today? They still live on in their lovely island home. Seen from the air in summer, with its hundreds of lakes, each a different shade of blue and each set in a big patch of golden moss, Kikerktak looks like an enchanted island, guarded sometimes by a turquoise sea, sometimes by a white sea of floating ice, and sometimes by a sea of molten lead that looks as if it had just been poured. Across the island's wide plains the Kikerktarmiut wander to their hunting and fishing places; and along its shores they seal. No longer do they use stone age weapons; today they have rifles and nets and traps. At the Hudson's Bay Post they trade fox skins for many of the white man's goods—guns, ammunition, tea, tobacco, flour, sugar, and kerosene; even mirrors, stockings, printed dresses, and fleece-lined bloomers. But the Kikerktarmiut have not bartered away their heritage for these trimmings of another civilization. They are still the ancient and wise people they have always been.

In Gjoa Haven the children of the Kikerktarmiut go to school; they must learn to meet a changing world, for which they need reading, writing, spelling, arithmetic and geography. Everything possible is done to help them master their own language and cherish their own culture. School begins at 9:30 in the morning and runs for two hours, then for another two hours in the afternoon. Attendance is far from regular; sometimes pupils are off hunting with their parents, who depend on game for food, for weeks. It is these school children, however, and those coming after them, who must protect Kikerktak and keep it a fabled island. If they do this, they will be thanked by their own people and their names will be forever remembered: Naigayok, the lean; Kopilrok, the worm; Uyarait, the stones; Arnaktauyok, the good girl; Inurarjuk, the small man; Koiksak, seal buttock; Krangoar, the little goose; Siutinuar, the little ear; Angutitsiar, the nice boy; Okpik, the owl; Diktoa, thin ice; and countless others like them.

Selected Bibliography

Amundsen, Roald, *The Northwest Passage*. New York, E. P. Dutton and Company, 1908.

Back, George, *Narrative of the Arctic Land Expedition to the Mouth of the Great Fish River*. London, 1836.

Cyriax, Richard J., *Sir John Franklin's Last Arctic Expedition*. London, Methuen & Co. Ltd., 1939.

Franklin, John, *Narrative of a Journey to the Shores of the Polar Sea, in 1819-22*. London, 1823.

———, *Narrative of a Second Expedition to the Shores of the Polar Sea, in 1825-27*. London, 1828.

Gilder, William H., *Schwatka's Search*. New York, 1881.

Hall, Charles F., *Narrative of the Second Arctic Expedition made by Charles F. Hall*. J. E. Nourse, ed. Washington, 1879.

———, Manuscript journals and notebooks and diaries at the Smithsonian Institution, Washington, D.C.

Hudson's Bay Record Society, *Rae's Arctic Correspondence*. London, 1953.

Kennedy, William, *A Short Narrative of the Second Voyage of the Prince Albert, in search of Sir John Franklin*. London, 1853.

King, Richard, *Narrative of a Journey to the Arctic Ocean, in 1833-35*. London, 1836.

McClintock, Francis Leopold, *The Voyage of the* Fox *in the Arctic Seas*. 5th edition, London, 1859.

Markham, Albert Hastings, *Life of Sir John Franklin and the North-West Passage*. London, 1891.

Parry, William Edward, *Journal of a Voyage for the Discovery of a North-West Passage in 1819-20*. London, 1821.

————, *Journal of a Second Voyage in 1821-23.* London, 1824.

————, *Journal of a Third Voyage in 1824-25.* London, 1826.

Rasmussen, Knud, "The Netsilik Eskimos." *Report of the Fifth Thule Expedition,* Vol. VIII. Copenhagen, Nordis Forlag, 1931.

Ross, John, *Narrative of a Second Voyage in Search of a North-West Passage, 1829-33.* London, 1835.

Simpson, Alexander, *The Life and Travels of Thomas Simpson, the Arctic Discoverer.* London, 1845.

Simpson, Thomas, *Narrative of the Discoveries on the North Coast of America.* London, 1843.

Snow, William Parker, *Voyage of the* Prince Albert *in Search of Sir John Franklin.* London, 1851.

Stefansson, Vilhjalmur, *Unsolved Mysteries of the Arctic.* New York, Macmillan, 1939.

Woodward, Frances J., *Portrait of Jane—A Life of Lady Franklin.* London, Hodder and Stoughton, 1951.

POINT BARROW

GREEN-LAND

ALASKA

PACIFIC OCEAN

C A N A D A

U. S.

MELVILLE

McCLURE STR.

BANKS I.

MELVILL

VICTORIA

TO POINT BARROW

SIMPSON

N

W   E

S

PT. TURNAGAIN

DISMAL LAKES

Ft. Confidence

DEASE R.

CORONATION GULF

K

ARCTIC BAY

HOOD R.

MACKENZIE R.

GREAT BEAR L.

COPPERMINE R.

BATHURST INLET

B A R

L. BEECHEY

MUSK-OX L.

Ft. Enterprise

AYLMER L.

CLINTON COLDEN L.

YELLOWKNIFE R.

ARTILLERY L.

BA

Ft. Reliance

Miles

0   50   100   200

map by palacios

GREAT SLAVE L.

Ft. Resolution